Slingers and Sling Bullets in the Roman Civil Wars of the Late Republic, 90-31 BC

Slingers and Sling Bullets in the Roman Civil Wars of the Late Republic, 90-31 BC

Lawrence Keppie

ARCHAEOPRESS ARCHAEOLOGY

Archaeopress Publishing Ltd
Summertown Pavilion
18-24 Middle Way
Summertown
Oxford OX2 7LG
www.archaeopress.com

ISBN 978-1-80327-640-3
ISBN 978-1-80327-641-0 (e-Pdf)

© Lawrence Keppie and Archaeopress 2023

Cover: Silver coin (*stater*) issued at Aspendus, Southern Turkey, depicting a Greek slinger, c. 420-360 BC. Photo: © The Ashmolean, University of Oxford (HCR 6778).

All rights reserved. No part of this book may be reproduced, or transmitted, in any form or by any means, electronic, mechanical, photocopying or otherwise, without the prior written permission of the copyright owners.

This book is available direct from Archaeopress or from our website www.archaeopress.com

Contents

Preface v

Chapter 1: Slingers and slinging in the Roman world 1
   Introduction 1
   Slings, slingers and sling bullets 1
   Inscriptions on lead bullets 9
   Balearic slingers 10
   A case study: the siege of Numantia, 134-133 BC 12

Chapter 2: The Social War and the siege of Asculum, 90-89 BC 15

Chapter 3: Sulla, Sertorius and Caesar, 89-50 BC 23
   Quintus Sertorius 23
   Caesar in Gaul, 58-50 BC 30
   Sosus, King of Mauretania 33

Chapter 4: Civil war 1: Caesar against Pompey and his sons, 49-45 BC 35
   The battle of Ilerda, 49 BC 35
   Dyrrhachium and Pharsalus, 48 BC 39
   Campaigns in Africa and Spain, 46-45 BC 42
   The battle of Munda, 45 BC 44

Chapter 5: Civil war 2: Caesar's heirs and successors, 44-42 BC 47
   The battle of Mutina, 43 BC 47
   Events of 42 BC: Calabria, Sicily, Philippi 50

Chapter 6: The siege of Perusia, 41-40 BC 53

Chapter 7: From Perusia to Actium, 40-31 BC 62

Chapter 8: Slingers under the Roman Empire 66

Chapter 9: The role of slingers in battle and their effectiveness 74

Chapter 10: Conclusion 77

Reference 1: Glossary 82

Reference 2: Bibliography 83
   Epigraphic corpora 83
   References 83

Index 95

List of Figures

Figure 1. Lead bullets naming Gnaeus Pompeius Magnus, son of Pompey the Great, 45 BC. Museo Arqueológico de Osuna, Spain. Photo: © Dr J.H. Reid. 2

Figure 2. Scene from the Altar of Domitius Ahenobarbus, Rome, showing two legionaries and a cavalryman. The date is disputed: perhaps the end of the 2nd century BC. Musée du Louvre, Paris. Photo: Jastrow (2007). Wikimedia Commons. 3

Figure 3. Numantia, Spain. Clay sling bullets from Adolf Schulten's excavations of 1905-12. Photo: A. Schulten, *Numantia II. Die Stadt Numantia*, 1931, München: Tafel 38B. 5

Figure 4. Front and side of a clay mould for lead bullets found in the Rue Saint-Martin, Paris. After Poux and Guyard. Scale 1:1. 6

Figure 5. Numantia, Spain. Plan of the town and siegeworks of 134-133 BC. After L. Keppie, *The Making of the Roman Army*, 1984, London: figure 15. 11

Figure 6. Numantia, Spain. Stone *ballista* balls from Adolf Schulten's excavations of 1905-12. Photo: A. Schulten, *Numantia III. Die Lager des Scipio*, 1927, München: Tafel 53. 13

Figure 7. Italy, showing places mentioned in the text. 14

Figure 8. Asculum (Ascoli Piceno, Italy). Course of the Castellano tributary at the Ponte di Cecco. The bridge, of Roman Republican or Augustan date, was reconstructed in the 1960s following wartime demolition. Photo: Pampuco. Wikimedia Commons. Licence: CC BY-SA 4.0 16

Figure 9. Lead sling bullets from Asculum and vicinity, 90-89 BC. After Zangemeister. Scale 1:1 17

Figure 10. Row of five slingers on a stone relief at Asculum (Ascoli Piceno, Italy). Museo Archeologico Statale di Ascoli Piceno. Photo: Cast in the Museo della Civiltà Romana, Rome. © Roma, Sovrintendenza Capitolina ai Beni Culturali. 19

Figure 11. Silver *denarius* depicting L. Cornelius Sulla, issued in 54 BC by his grandson. The coin legend reads: SVLLA·COS (Sulla consul). Photo: © The Hunterian, University of Glasgow (GLAHM 22407). 22

Figure 12. Pompeii, The Anglo-American Project. Excavation in progress close to the Herculaneum Gate, 2004. Photo: © The late Margaret J. Robb. Courtesy of Dr R.F.J. Jones 24

Figure 13. Lead sling bullets of the Late Republic, from Renieblas (near Numantia, Spain), naming Quintus Sertorius (no. 1); Volubilis (Morocco), naming Sosus, King of Mauretania; the other side shows what may be a stylised lightning-bolt (no. 2); Numantia (Spain), recording in Greek the Aetolian slingers (no. 3); Apsorus (Croatia), from a suggested siege

Figure 14. France, Belgium, Holland, Germany (Roman Gaul), showing places mentioned in the text. 27
Figure 15. Alesia (Alise-Sainte-Reine, France). 28
Figure 16. South of France, showing places mentioned in the text. Note: 1. Altès; 2. Saint-Affrique; 3. Saint-Pargoire; 4. Les Petites Caisses; 5. Saint-Blaise; 6. La Cloche. 29
Figure 17. North Africa, showing places mentioned in the text. 29
Figure 18. Lead sling bullets of the Late Republic, from Paris (no. 1), Alesia (nos 2-4), Le Mas d'Agenais (no. 5), Saint-Pargoire (no. 6), Sicily (no. 7), L'Ermitage d'Agen (no. 8). After Poux and Robin (no. 1), Sievers (nos 2-4), Feugère (nos 5-6), Costabile (no. 7), Verdin (no. 8). Scale 1:1. 32
Figure 19. Spain and Portugal, showing places mentioned in the text 34
Figure 20. Lead sling bullets, Spain, 49-45 BC, from Ilerda (no. 1), Menorca (no. 2), Urso (no. 3), Cerro de las Balas (nos 4-5). After López Vilar (no. 1), De Nicolàs (no. 2); Díaz Ariño (no. 3), Pina Polo and Zanier (nos 4-5). Scale 1:1. 36
Figure 21. North-Eastern Spain, to illustrate events in 133-49 BC. Note: 1. Prades; 2. Picamoixons. 37
Figure 22. Silver *denarius*, showing an elephant trampling a serpent, 49-48 BC. The coin legend reads: CAESAR. Photo: © The Hunterian, University of Glasgow (GLAHM 22426). 38
Figure 23. Greece, showing places mentioned in the text. 39
Figure 24. Siegelines constructed by Caesar and by Pompey at Dyrrhachium (Durrës, Albania), 48 BC. The siting of individual forts, marked here by dots, is largely hypothetical. After L. Keppie, *The Making of the Roman Army*, 1984, London: figure 31). 40
Figure 25. Southern Spain, to illustrate events in 49-45 BC. Note: 1. Alcalá de Guadaíra; 2. Lantejuela; 3. Puebla de Cazalla. 43
Figure 26. Silver *denarius* depicting Julius Caesar, 44 BC. The coin legend reads: CAESAR·DICT·PERPETVO (Caesar, dictator for life). Photo: © The Hunterian, University of Glasgow (GLAHM 22531). 45
Figure 27. Northern Italy, showing location of Mutina (Modena). 48
Figure 28. Gold *aureus* depicting Octavian, 42 BC. The coin legend reads: C·CAESAR·III·VIR·R·P·C (Gaius Caesar, Triumvir for the ordering of the state). Photo: © The Hunterian, University of Glasgow (GLAHM 22579). 49
Figure 29. Silver *denarius* naming Q. Salvidienus Rufus and showing a lightning-bolt, 40 BC. The coin legend reads: Q·SALVIVS·IMP·COS·DESIG (Quintus Salvius, saluted as victorious commander, consul designate). Photo: © The Hunterian, University of Glasgow (GLAHM 22687). 50
Figure 30. Sicily and Calabria (Italy), to illustrate events in 42-36 BC. Note: 1. Mylae; 2. Naulochus; 3. Rhegium; 4. Leucopetra. 51

Figure 31. Perusia (Perugia, Italy). Panoramic view from the North-West, showing the Basilica of San Domenico (centre), with the bell-tower of the Abbazia of San Pietro further towards the right. Photo: trolvag. Wikimedia Commons. Licence: CC BY-SA 3.0 Unported. 54

Figure 32. Lead sling bullets from Perusia (Italy), 41-40 BC. After Keppie (nos 1-3, front, 5-8; Benedetti (nos 3 back, 4). Scale 1:1. 55

Figure 33. Lead sling bullets from Perusia (Italy), 41-40 BC. After Benedetti (nos 1, 3); Keppie nos 2, 4-6). Scale 1:1. 56

Figure 34. Silver *denarius* depicting Lucius Antonius, 41 BC. The coin legend reads: L·ANTONIVS·COS (Lucius Antonius, consul). Photo: Classical Numismatic Group. Inc. Wikimedia Commons. Licence: CC BY-SA 3.0 Unported. 59

Figure 35. Lead sling bullet from Perusia (Italy), 41-40 BC. After Benedetti. Scale 2:1. 60

Figure 36. Gold *aureus* depicting Sextus Pompeius, 42-40 BC. The coin legend reads: MAG·PIVS·IMP·ITER (Magnus Pius, twice saluted victorious commander). Photo: © The Hunterian, University of Glasgow (GLAHM 22653) 62

Figure 37. Silver *denarius* issued by Mark Antony, 32-31 BC. The obverse (above) shows a galley, the reverse (below) an eagle between two standards, celebrating his legion V. The coin legend reads (obverse): ANT·AVG·IIIVIR·R·P·C (Antonius, augur, Triumvir for the ordering of the state); (reverse): LEG V (legion V) Photo: © The Hunterian, University of Glasgow (GLAHM 22733). 63

Figure 38. Tombstone from Rome, naming the slinger Epitynchanus, AD 100 or later. After De Minicis, *Sulle antiche ghiande*, 1844, Roma: tabula 1. 67

Figure 39. Trajan's Column, Rome. A slinger and a stone-thrower. Photo: C. Cichorius, *Die Reliefs der Traiansäule,* 1896, Berlin: scene lxvi. Courtesy of Glasgow University Library. 68

Figure 40. Trajan's Column, Rome. A stone-thrower poised to cast a stone. Photo: C. Cichorius, *Die Reliefs der Traiansäule*. 1896, Berlin: scene lxxii. Courtesy of Glasgow University Library. 69

Figure 41. Trajan's Column, Rome. A slinger viewed from behind. Photo: C. Cichorius, *Die Reliefs der Traiansäule*, 1896, Berlin: scene cxiii. Courtesy of Glasgow University Library. 70

Figure 42. Column of Marcus Aurelius, Rome. A group of bearded slingers. Photo: E. Petersen, A. von Domaszewski and G. Calderini, *Die Marcus-Säule auf Piazza Colonna in Rom*, 1896, München: scene x. Courtesy of Glasgow University Library 72

Preface

Some books on the Roman army make little or no mention of slingers who were an element in the Roman armed forces over many centuries. The present monograph seeks to redress the balance. The emphasis is on the historical and epigraphic evidence, set against the political and military events of the period 90-31 BC.

For their assistance and advice during the preparation of this monograph, I should particularly like to thank the late Prof. J.N. Adams (All Souls College, Oxford), Dr J.D. Bateson and J. Ericsson (The Hunterian, University of Glasgow), Prof. D.J. Breeze and Dr T.S. Brown (University of Edinburgh), Prof. R.P.H. Green (University of Glasgow), Prof. Á. Morillo Cerdán (Universidad Complutense de Madrid), Dr Regine Müller (Pohlheim), Prof. J. Osborne (Carleton University, Ottawa) and Dr Silvia Pellegrini (Museo Civico Archeologico, Modena). I am especially grateful to Dr J.H. Reid (Trimontium Trust, Melrose) for many insights into slinging, often as a result of his practical experiments. The discovery in 2015-16 of numerous lead bullets by Dr Reid and A. Nicholson at the hillfort of Burnswark (Dumfries and Galloway) reignited my interest in this category of ancient evidence. Dr Marenne Zandstra (Museum Het Valkhof, Nijmegen) kindly made available passages from her unpublished doctoral thesis. For access to the collections of bullets in their care, I thank Gemma Plumpton and colleagues (The Ashmolean, Oxford) and Antonio Fernández Ugalde (Museo Histórico Municipal, Écija). Prof. D.J. Breeze and Prof. A.M. Small kindly read an early version of the text, to my advantage.

The following chapters were largely written in 2019-22 during periods of lockdown and restrictions imposed by Covid 19. In searching out academic papers in journals not then accessible to me, I was fortunate in being able to enlist the help of Prof. Y. Le Bohec (Lille), Dr A. Montgomery (London), Valerie Scott (British School at Rome) and Dr Helen Whitehouse (The Ashmolean, Oxford). I subsequently made extensive use of the substantial resources of Glasgow University Library and the Bodleian Library, Oxford. Mike Schurer and his colleagues at Archaeopress saw the manuscript through to publication with their customary skill. The maps were prepared by the author. With a few exceptions Roman place-names are given in their Latin forms, with the modern name (if different) in brackets. On the maps, modern place-names are shown in Italics.

The lead bullets illustrated below (Figures 9, 13, 18, 20, 32, 33, 35) were redrawn by the author from published sources which are acknowledged in the captions. Individual bullets are reproduced here at approximately 1:1, except for Figure 33 which is at 2:1. Stefania Peterlini (British School at Rome) facilitated the acquisition of an image from the Museo della Civiltà Romana, Rome, and Rosanna van den Bogaerde one from The Ashmolean, Oxford. All the bullets illustrated are identified in the text. In the footnotes bibliographic items are listed in chronological order of publication.

Chapter 1

Slingers and slinging in the Roman world

Introduction

The first century BC was characterised at Rome by political turmoil, often leading to civil war. The protagonists were chiefly members of the senatorial class; many paid for their choices of allegiance with their lives. The wars involved Italy and many parts of the wider Mediterranean world.

Before the Social War of 90-89 BC Rome's army consisted of legions of Roman citizens supported by contingents of Allies (the *Socii*). After the subsequent granting of Roman citizenship to the Allies, the number of legions grew; there were normally about 14 in existence each year, often more.[1] Legionaries at this time wore mail shirts and plumed helmets, and carried oval shields (Figure 2). During periods of civil war their number substantially increased. Service in the legions was for a minimum of six years, which might be extended to a maximum of 16, undertaken between the ages of 17 and 46. The legions at this time were recruited almost exclusively from Italy. Soldiers sought and often obtained rewards on completion of their service, sometimes in cash but increasingly land at colonies in Italy or in the provinces.[2]

In support of the legions on campaign during the Late Republic were contingents of cavalry, light infantry, archers and slingers usually drawn from conquered territories and allied communities and kingdoms.[3] No naval squadrons were kept in permanent commission by the Romans themselves at this time; they drew warships and their crews from allied states chiefly in the eastern Mediterranean.[4]

Slings, slingers and sling bullets

The use of slings was common throughout the ancient Mediterranean world both in hunting and in warfare, with bullets (*glandes*) made of stone, clay or lead. The Greek city-states made extensive use of slingers in their many wars,[5] as did the Etruscans

---

[1] Brunt 1971: 446.
[2] Keppie 1983.
[3] Harmand 1967: 43.
[4] Kromayer 1897: 432; Starr 1941: 1; Harmand 1967: 213.
[5] Pritchett 1991: 1.

Figure 1. Lead bullets naming Gnaeus Pompeius Magnus, son of Pompey the Great, 45 BC. Museo Arqueológico de Osuna, Spain. Photo: © Dr J.H. Reid.

and other peoples in Italy.[6] The Romans had included slingers (*funditores*) in their army from earliest times.[7]

There is a long tradition of modern scholarship in the publishing of sling bullets. In 1844 Gaetano De Minicis assembled a substantial corpus of Roman lead bullets, with scale drawings.[8] In 1885 an authoritative catalogue of inscribed lead bullets of the Roman period was published by Karl Zangemeister, with commentaries in Latin.[9] The comprehensive survey in 1972 by Bernard Henry deserves to be better known.[10] In 1990 Thomas Völling valuably listed and discussed well over 6000 lead bullets and 10,000 clay bullets recovered from Roman sites.[11] Völling helpfully identified six

---

[6] Lead and clay bullets recovered long ago from a cemetery area outside the town of Hatria (Adria) in the Po delta (*Notizie degli Scavi di Antichitá* 1879: 96; Sovernigo 2018), though sometimes considered Roman (Fogolari and Scarfi 1970: 89 tavola 71.2), could belong to an earlier phase in the history of the town. A helmeted slinger in a linen corselet is depicted in a battle-scene on a Late Etruscan limestone sarcophagus at Clusium (Chiusi) in Etruria (Herbig 1952: 18 no. 14 Tafel 48; Völling 1990: 30 Abbildung 9).
[7] Livy 1.43.7.
[8] De Minicis 1844 with Marengo 2015.
[9] Zangemeister 1885. See also Fougères 1896a; 1896b; Liebenam 1910a; 1910b.
[10] Henry 1972. A typescript copy is held in the Bodleian Library, Oxford.
[11] Völling 1990: 34, 38. See also the important studies by Greep 1987 and Rihll 2009. A series of papers by

Figure 2. Scene from the Altar of Domitius Ahenobarbus, Rome, showing two legionaries and a cavalryman. The date is disputed: perhaps the end of the 2nd century BC. Musée du Louvre, Paris. Photo: Jastrow (2007). Wikimedia Commons.

different types of lead bullets (Types I-VI), based on their shapes;[12] his classification has been widely adopted. Often several of Völling's Types are found together at a single well-dated site, indicating perhaps that groups of slingers were casting lead bullets independently.

Slingers were lightly armed, protection being sacrificed to mobility. They wore neither helmets nor body armour.[13] The geographer Strabo writing under Augustus records that slingers from the Balearic Islands (below p. 10) went naked into battle but carried a goatskin shield and an iron-tipped spear.[14] Hannibal's brother Mago is described as equipped with sword, bow and Balearic sling.[15]

W.B. Griffiths (1989; 1992; Griffiths and Carrick 1994) encompasses slinging, slings and stone-throwing.
[12] Völling 1990: 34 with Abbildung 19. For recent critiques of his Types, see Müller 2018: 37 Tabelle 3; Schinco and Small 2020: 96.
[13] For their arms, dress and equipment under the Empire, see below p. 66.
[14] Strabo *Geog.* 3.5.1.
[15] Sil. Ital. *Pun.* 7.296.

We are helped in our understanding by the depiction of slingers on coins, mosaics, vase-paintings and relief sculpture.[16] A slinger features on the Greek silver coinage of Aspendus in Southern Turkey (Front Cover), in the 5th and 4th centuries BC.[17] A Greek white-ground *lecythos* (oil flask) dating to the 5th century BC depicts an Amazonian warrior armed with bow, sling and two spears.[18] Only one depiction of slingers (Figure 10) is datable to our period (below p. 20); others are later in date, but valuable as showing slingers in battle (Figures 39-42).

The slings (*fundae*) were commonly of leather but other materials are reported.[19] Each sling consisted of two lengths of cord linked by a pouch. Some examples survive from antiquity.[20] The bullet was gripped in the slinger's left hand, the two cords in the right, one of which was attached to the slinger's thumb.[21] Balearic slingers (for whom see below p. 10) carried three slings of different lengths, by which they could achieve varying distances.[22] The slingers swung their slings up to three times round their head, before letting go one end of the cord.[23]

The bullets themselves (*glandes*) were of stone, baked clay or lead.[24] Attention focuses on lead bullets, which sometimes bear Latin inscriptions (see below p. 9), but stone and clay were in regular use, increasingly so under the Empire. Bullets are not inherently datable except when linked to known events by the inscriptions they bear or by their findspots.

Bullets of stone, assuredly the oldest form, could be picked up from river-beds and on hillsides.[25] The Biblical shepherd-boy David 'chose him five smooth stones out of the brook, and put them in a shepherd's bag, which he had, even in a scrip; and his sling was in his hand,' when he advanced to confront the fully-armed Goliath.'[26] Sometimes the stones were much heavier, as for example at Lomba do Canho, Spain (below p. 26), where they weighed as much as 191 gms. Balearic slingers were known for their ability to sling heavy stones.[27]

---

[16] Völling 1990: Abbildungen 5, 9, 14-16.
[17] Kraay and Hirmer 1966: nos 663-65; Pritchett 1991: 37.
[18] Von Bothmer 1957: 202 plate 84.1.
[19] Strabo *Geog.* 3.5.1. See Griffiths 1989: 256; Griffiths and Carrick 1994.
[20] Wild 1998; Granger-Taylor 2012: 73 with figure 6.11. A fragmentary tombstone from Xanten, now in the Rheinisches Landesmuseum, Bonn, shows a legionary whose left hand holds a tube-shaped object suggested as a sling (Bauchhenss 1978: 30 no. 10).
[21] Völling 1990: 29-30 Abbildungen 6, 8.
[22] Diod. Sic. 5.18.3; Strabo *Geog.* 3.5.1.
[23] Sil. Ital. *Pun.* 1.313. See below p. 74 for the range and impact of bullets.
[24] The word *glandes* literally means 'acorns'. The acorn-shape (Völling 1990: Type V) is currently restricted to Burnswark hillfort in Southern Scotland, which was attacked by a Roman army c. AD 142, and some local sites on or near Hadrian's Wall. Perhaps a supervisor interpreted too literally an instruction to manufacture *glandes*.
[25] Livy 1.43.7, 38.20.1.
[26] *I Samuel* 17.40 (King James Version). David's story is taken up again below p. 76.
[27] Diod. Sic. 19.109.

Figure 3. Numantia, Spain. Clay sling bullets from Adolf Schulten's excavations of 1905-12. Photo: A. Schulten, *Numantia II. Die Stadt Numantic*, 1931, München: Tafel 38B.

Throwing stones by hand had a long pedigree.[28] In the Roman period, they sometimes weighed about one *libra* pound (0.329 kg),[29] hence the Latin name *libritores* to describe their users.[30] Such stones were about the size of a cricket ball but were twice as heavy.

---
[28] Pritchett 1991: 1, 65.
[29] Veg. *De Re Mil.* 2.23.
[30] Tac. *Ann.* 2.20, 13.39.

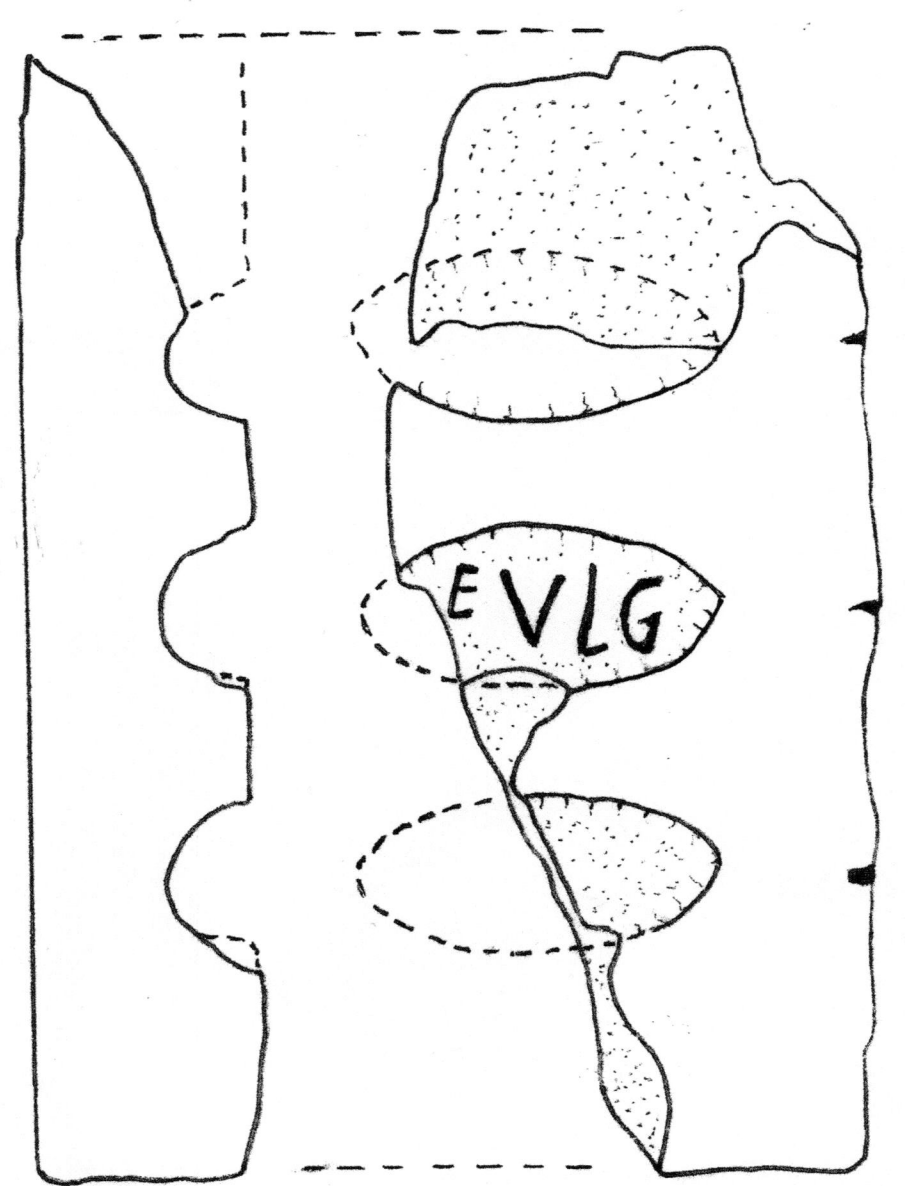

Figure 4. Side and front of a clay mould for lead bullets found in the Rue Saint-Martin, Paris. After Poux and Guyard. Scale 1:1.

A strong arm was a basic requirement for a stone-thrower.[31] Slingers and stone-throwers often acted in combination. It is not always clear in some literary accounts whether stones were being slung or thrown.

Bullets of baked clay have survived in quantity at Paestum in Italy (below p. 23), at Numantia in Spain (below p. 12), and at Lambaesis in Algeria (below p. 71). Clay bullets were widely used in Celtic western Europe. Some resemble lead bullets in size and shape; others are much larger and heavier. Clay bullets were in use by the Gauls when Caesar fought them in 58-50 BC; heated clay bullets were directed by the Gauls against Quintus Cicero's camp among the Nervii in 54 BC.[32] Völling distinguished three Types of clay bullets.[33]

Lead bullets had been in widespread use in warfare by the Greek city-states, and the Romans employed them from at least the later third century BC onwards.[34] Some bore Latin inscriptions (see below). Lead bullets were manufactured in clay moulds, each accommodating up to a dozen bullets in oval hollows. Moulds could be either univalve or bivalve (single or double), producing bullets which were either 'monofacial' or 'bifacial', with inscriptions on one or both sides. Large numbers of moulds must have been required; a few have survived.[35] The lead itself needed to be sourced, transported in the form of ingots, melted and poured.[36]

Of particular interest is a fragmentary clay mould for lead bullets found by excavation at Paris in 1991 (Figure 4).[37] A dating in the early 1st century AD is proposed. It is the only mould of this period known to me which bears an inscription, appearing to read FVLG, i.e. *fulgur* ('lightning'). The word is inscribed in only one of the three surviving oval cavities. Many bullets of this period bear an embossed lightning-bolt image (see Figure 32.1, 3).

The surviving lead bullets are often almond-shaped and are generally 35-55mms long.[38] Others have flattened sides,[39] or occasionally a flat end.[40] Some of those naming Gnaeus Pompeius the Younger (below p. 44) are biconical (Figures 1, 20.3). Boat-shapes found at several sites result from the use of univalve moulds (see above).

---

[31] Sil. Ital. *Pun.* 1. 317.
[32] Caes. *BG* 5.43.
[33] Völling 1990: 38 Abbildung 22.
[34] Henry 1972: volume 1, 91; Völling 1990: 25, 35.
[35] Zangemeister 1885: pp. x-xii; Robinson 1942: 419; Korfmann 1973; Völling 1990: 40; Pritchett 1991: 45 footnote 80.
[36] Lead is easily workable, melting at the relatively low temperature of 327.5 degrees Celsius. For some lead ingots of Augustan date, see Bode *et al.* 2021. See now 'The Corpus of Roman Lead Ingots', hosted by the University of Cologne.
[37] *AE* 2000, 974. See Poux and Guyard 1999; Poux 2008: 370.
[38] For a discussion of shapes see Sievers 2001: 173; Fontenla Ballesta 2005: 69; Rihll 2009: 154; Schinco and Small 2020: 95.
[39] Moralejo Ordax and Saavedra 2016: figure 4-6.
[40] Brouquier-Reddé 1997: 280 figure 3; Fontenla Ballesta 2005.

Some bullets show cuts and notches, which can reflect damage caused by impact or result from the moulding process. Though small holes in some lead bullets could have held poison, more probably they were intended to produce a whistling sound.[41] Most lead bullets weigh between c. 40 and c.70 gms, but some are much heavier. The lead bullets from Cerro de las Balas, Spain (below p. 44), datable to 45 BC, exhibit a very wide range of weights, between 22 and 103gms. Collections of bullets formed on the Balearic island of Menorca range from 20gms up to 120gms in weight (below p. 10).

At some sites the surviving bullets can be grouped into definite categories related to the Roman weight system,[42] and it has been suggested that distinct calibres existed across the Graeco-Roman world.[43] Nevertheless, the evidence for the Late Republic seems insufficient to indicate a widespread weight-standard consistently applied. The size of bullets at any site will be determined by the capacity of the moulds used. At Perusia (below p. 54) bullets inscribed with the name of the legate Salvidienus Rufus are of a consistent weight, while those naming the centurion Apidius (from a number of different moulds) have a wide range of weights; those carrying the enigmatic lettering LVFINASIA, which have a single find-location (below p. 58), weighed between 37 and 52gms and had been cast from several moulds.[44]

Lead isotope analysis has been undertaken on bullets from Britain, Spain, Portugal, Belgium and Italy.[45] Spain was throughout a principal source for the lead used. The range, velocity and accuracy of bullets have been the subject of intense modern study.

The lifespan of bullets was often short. Individual slingers could have carried only a relatively small number over long distances. Rather, they were manufactured in quantity as circumstances required (see below p. 42). When the Roman fort at Velsen, Netherlands, came under attack in AD 28, lead bullets were apparently shot off by the fort's unknown defenders as fast as they could be made.[46]

During the nineteenth century considerable doubt was expressed over the genuineness of inscribed lead bullets, especially finds reported at Asculum (Ascoli Piceno, Italy) and Perusia (Perugia, Italy), where numerous crude forgeries were soon produced.[47] Genuine bullets have sometimes been given inscriptions only in modern times. We hear less about forgeries nowadays, as discoveries have often come from excavation or fieldwork.

---

[41] Caes. *Bell. Afr.* 83. See Reid and Nicholson 2019: 470. Stone bullets too made a sound when travelling through the air (Sil. Ital. *Pun.* 1.317).
[42] E.g. at Pompeii (Burns 2004: 2), Burnswark (Reid and Nicholson 2019: 468 with fig. 5) and Alesia (Poux 2008: 369).
[43] Ble Gimeno 2016: 182; cf. Noguera *et al.* 2022: 21.
[44] Benedetti 2012a: nos 9-13, 17-22, 44-55.
[45] Müller *et al.* 2014; Gomes *et al.* 2017; Paridaens *et al.* 2020.
[46] Bosman 1995.
[47] Zangemeister 1885: 88; Laffi 1981; Polita 2007: 15; Rihll 2009: 156; Benedetti 2012a: 36 tavola 31.

Inscriptions on lead bullets

The Romans began to inscribe lead bullets at the time of the Second Punic War in the late 3rd century BC.[48] The bullets were 'inscribed' in the sense that, for the most part, the lettering was cut into their moulds, then cast so as to be embossed on the final product. They were not casually incised by soldiers in their off-duty moments.[49] The texts needed to be inscribed 'retrograde' into the moulds, but not all the makers remembered to do so. However, large numbers of surviving lead bullets bear no inscriptions and within a single group only a minority may bear any inscription. Occasionally the lettering has been stamped on to the bullets rather than inscribed in a mould.[50]

The earliest inscribed lead bullets name Roman magistrates,[51] and this practice continued into the Late Republic.[52] Bullets can also name individual legions or centurions (below, pp. 18, 48-54), as well as civilian manufacturers (below p. 57) and, it seems, municipalities (below, p. 45). On occasion they carry insults and ribald messages aimed at opposing commanders (below, pp. 49, 58), continuing long-established Greek practice. Despite the fact that during the civil wars of the Late Republic upwards of 60 legions were in service at various times, and are attested epigraphically up to XLI,[53] the highest number securely inscribed on a surviving bullet is XV.

The Latin texts on lead bullets were truncated to the minimum lettering needed for comprehension. For example, the word *legio* ('legion') is often abbreviated to the single letter L.[54] The letters could also be ligatured (linked together), again with a view to maximising the information to be imparted. The Latin inscriptions were almost always written in capital letters, not the cursive script employed for everyday communication. Words are generally separated by interpuncts, placed halfway up the letters, i.e. 'medial' interpuncts. Symbols could also be inscribed, including lightning-bolts, alluding to the swift flight of the bullets through the air.[55] In a few cases the necessarily brief messages defy modern interpretation, but were presumably readily understood at the time, both by their makers and the intended recipients.

---

[48] *ILLRP* 1088. See Manganaro 2000: 129; Benedetti 2012a: 32. Clay bullets too were occasionally inscribed (Manganaro 2000: 126).
[49] For exceptions see Benedetti 2012a: no. 33 (here Figure 35); *CIL* I² 887 (here Figure 13.4).
[50] See Pina Polo and Zanier 2006: 54 (Cerro de las Balas); Perea Yébenes 1997 (Córdoba); Rageth, Zanier and Klein 2010 (Graubünden).
[51] *ILLRP* 1088; Manganaro 2000: 129; Benedetti 2012a: 32.
[52] See below p. 33 for bullets naming a client king. For a sling bullet naming Tissaphernes, Persian satrap of Lydia 413-397 BC, see Foss 1975.
[53] Brunt 1971: 475 with *ILS* 2230-2231.
[54] Henry 1974. See Figures 9.4, 21.6, 25.4, 32.5-7, 33.3,5.
[55] An eye-motif is shown with the numerals XII on bullets at Ilerda, Spain (López Vilar 2013b: 455 figura 7; Noguera *et al.* 2018: 899 figure 3). For political watchwords on bullets issued by Quintus Sertorius in Spain, see below p. 24).

Balearic slingers

Slingers from the Balearic Islands (Mallorca, Menorca, Ibiza) were famed throughout the Mediterranean world.[56] They excelled in shooting both stone and lead bullets, having practised since childhood.[57] They could sling extremely heavy stones, weighing up to one Greek *mina* (0.435 kg).[58] Long employed by the Carthaginians, Balearic slingers accompanied Hannibal on his march from Spain to Italy and were present on his side at the subsequent battles.[59]

The Balearic islanders resisted Roman conquest of the islands in 123 BC; the consul Q. Caecilius Metellus (subsequently *Baliaricus*) fitted hides above the decks of his ships to protect soldiers and oarsmen from sling bullets, as he approached by sea.[60] Thereafter their slingers were available to serve Rome, which they did in the war against Jugurtha, King of Numidia, in 105 BC.[61] Presumably they were active too in the Social War of 90-89 BC but their activities are not reported.

Excavation of a Roman military installation at Sanisera (Sanitja) on the Balearic island of Menorca, in use between the conquest of 123 BC and 45 BC, yielded over 120 lead bullets and some stone bullets.[62] All were presumably of local origin. Some have distinctive shapes. The substantial collections of lead bullets assembled locally on the Balearic island of Ibiza weigh between 22 and 120gms, and can be of unusual shapes.[63]

In 57 BC Caesar counted slingers from the Balearic Islands among his army,[64] but his later references to slingers in Gaul do not report their homelands.[65] No extant lead bullet names Balearic slingers. By contrast, the slingers from Aetolia in Greece serving at Numantia in 133 BC (see below) inscribed the geographical name on their bullets in the time-honoured Greek fashion. It was perhaps a matter of literacy.

---

[56] De Nicolás Mascaró 1983; Pritchett 1991: 24; Planes Palau and Madrid Aznar 1994; Zucca 1998: 69; Domínguez Monedero 2005. For the anatomical consequences of prolonged slinging, observed in the shoulder joints of slingers of an earlier age on the Balearic island of Menorca, see Cameron 1934: 209; cf. Greep 1987: 197 fn. 77.
[57] Diod. Sic. 5.18.3; Veg. *De Re Mil.* 1.16.
[58] Diod. Sic. 19.109.
[59] Polyb. 3.72, 3.83; Livy 22.37, 22.49, 27.2.6; Sil.Ital. *Pun.* 1.314, 8.521.
[60] Strabo *Geog.* 3.5.1.
[61] Sall. *Jug.* 105.1-2.
[62] Contreras Rodrigo *et al.* 2006; Müller *et al.* 2014. The lead finds from the site were admirably published by Müller 2018.
[63] Planes Palau and Madrid Aznar 1994: 20. Some bullets were recovered when its harbour was dredged.
[64] Caes. *BG* 2.7. In the following pages, Book 8 of the *Gallic War*, and the *Alexandrian*, *African* and *Spanish Wars* are ascribed to Caesar, even though it has long been accepted that they were composed by his 'continuators'.
[65] Caes. *BG* 2.10, 19, 24, 8.40.

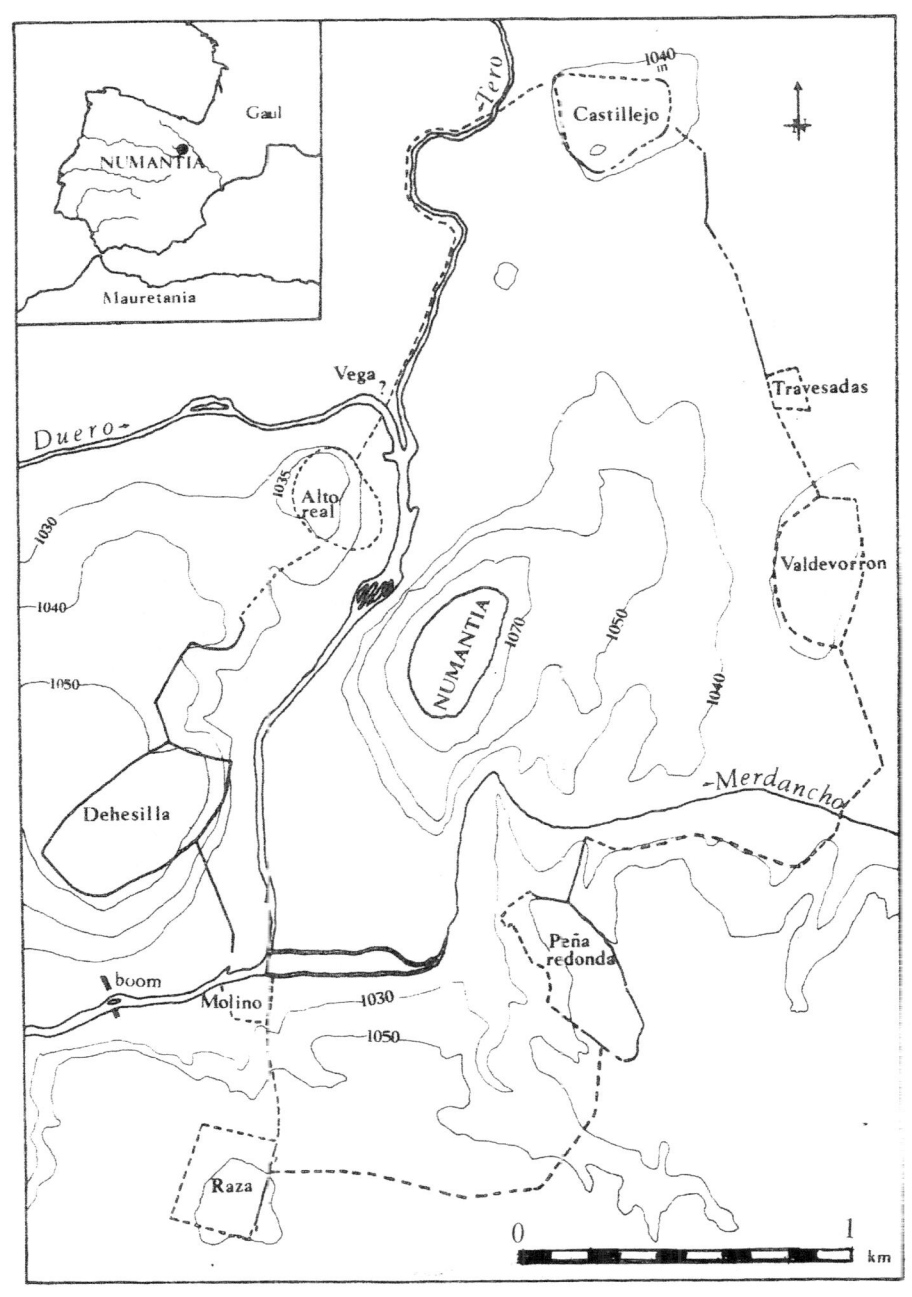

Figure 5. Numantia, Spain. Plan of the town and siegeworks of 134-133 BC. After L. Keppie, *The Making of the Roman Army*, 1984, London: figure 15.

A case study: the siege of Numantia, 134-133 BC

In 134 BC Scipio Aemilianus, the conqueror of Carthage, was elected consul and despatched to Spain with the remit to end the long-running war against the Celtiberians of North-Central Spain, who had frustrated or defeated previous Roman commanders. Scipio laid siege to the hilltop town of Numantia, constructing a nine-km long circumvallation and building a series of forts along its course to house his army (Figure 5),[66] which consisted of two legions together with allied contingents. Archers and slingers were placed along the circumvallation, perhaps in the regularly spaced wooden towers.[67] According to Frontinus, Scipio Aemilianus 'distributed archers and slingers not only among all his cohorts but among all his centuries too'.[68] He was also able to deploy 12 elephants 'with their associated archers and slingers', which had been brought from North Africa by the young Numidian prince Jugurtha.[69] The historian Appian could be referring to the very small number of soldiers who were sometimes placed in the 'towers' on top of elephants,[70] or more probably he means the groups of archers and slingers which sometimes accompanied elephants on campaign.[71]

Extensive excavation of the town and the forts on the circumvallation at Numantia was undertaken by Adolf Schulten in 1905-12. Small finds included weaponry, sling bullets and *ballista* balls, the latter found mainly in the Scipionic forts (Figure 6).[72] A total of some 320 bullets was recovered during Schulten's excavations, in the town and at the associated forts. Of these, some 23 were of lead, 19 of them found in the town, more probably shot by the attackers than by the Numantines.[73] Attention has focused on ten bullets bearing the Greek lettering Αἰτωλῶν, in the genitive case, 'belonging to the Aetolians', which bring before us slingers from Aetolia (Figure 13.3), a mountainous region of Central Greece, north-west of Delphi.[74] The Aetolians were skilled slingers.[75] A long-standing client-patron relationship with Scipio Aemilianus has been proposed to account for their unexpected presence at Numantia.[76] Five such bullets were recovered during excavations in the town, four somewhere south of Numantia, perhaps in one of the forts, and one at the Renieblas complex several kilometres to the east.[77] The distribution confirms that the Aetolians served on the Roman side during the siege. Those found in the forts could identify places where the

---

[66] Campbell 2005: 8.
[67] App. *Hisp.* 90-92.
[68] Front. *Strat.* 4.7.27.
[69] App. *Hisp.* 89.
[70] Polyaenus *Strat.* 8.23.5.
[71] Diod. Sic. 19.27.5, 19.82.3.
[72] Schulten 1927: 264 Tafel 53.
[73] Schulten 1927: 256 Tafeln 35.18, 20; 47.6; Völling 1990: 52 no. 89; Luik 2002: 85 Abbildung 95 nos 257-59.
[74] *SEG* 1996, 1371; *AE* 1996, 900. See González 1996; Gómez-Pantoja and Morales Hernández 2008.
[75] Strabo *Geog.* 8.3.33.
[76] González 1996; Gómez-Pantoja and Morales Hernández 2008: 52.
[77] Gómez-Pantoja and Morales Hernández 2008: 40.

Figure 6. Numantia, Spain. Stone *ballista* balls from Adolf Schulten's excavations of 1905-12. Photo: A. Schulten, *Numantia III. Die Lager des Scipio*, 1927, München: Tafel 53.

Aetolians were based. The users of the much more numerous clay bullets (Figure 3), some 300 in all, remain uncertain.[78] As almost all came from destruction layers in the town, they could represent the defenders' unused ammunition. The interpretation favoured by Schulten would see them shot into the town by the besiegers.[79]

The Numantines sallied out early in the siege to attack the circumvallation.[80] However, the literary sources do not record any pitched battle or an assault on the town's walls. Rather the besiegers waited for hunger to take its toll. The town was eventually reduced by starvation after an eight-month siege, with many of the defenders committing suicide. The town was destroyed and its buildings levelled.[81] Numantia is assuredly the Masada of Spain.[82]

---

[78] Schulten 1931: 269 Tafel 38B nos 42-44.
[79] Schulten 1927: 256.
[80] App. *Hisp.* 93-94.
[81] Schulten 1931: 171.
[82] Keppie 1984: 47.

Figure 7. Italy, showing places mentioned in the text.

Chapter 2

The Social War and the siege of Asculum, 90-89 BC

The political events leading up to the Social War against Rome's Italian allies (the *Socii*), its course and its consequences have been extensively studied,[1] but our knowledge of individual military events remains sketchy. Very large numbers of soldiers were involved on both sides.

The war was sparked off by a massacre of Roman citizens at the town of Asculum (Ascoli Piceno), inland from Italy's Adriatic coast, and the seizure of their property. The town subsequently underwent a long siege by Roman forces. Asculum is an easily defensible site, difficult of access and surrounded by high mountains, at the junction of the River Truentus (Tronto) with its Castellano tributary, which both run through deep gorges (Figure 8). As a result defensive walls were needed only on its west and south-west sides.[2] The literary sources make no mention of slingers who, as we shall see, were present at the siege on both sides.

Sling bullets have been reported at Asculum from the early seventeenth century onwards (Figure 9).[3] In 1874-79 several thousand were recovered from the bed of the Castellano tributary, especially between the Ponte di Porta Maggiore and the adjacent Ponte di Cecco; they had become lodged in folds of the underlying tufa.[4] Karl Zangemeister, soon to be the author of the enduring monograph on inscribed sling bullets, travelled from Berlin to Asculum in 1877 at the bidding of the eminent historian Theodor Mommsen, making him in effect an eyewitness in the immediate aftermath of these discoveries.[5] Writing in association with local antiquary, painter and librarian Giulio Gabrielli, his assessments are particularly valuable. Zangemeister made numerous line-drawings of the bullets. A large number of forgeries were soon produced locally.[6]

Later finds have included 521 lead bullets uncovered east of the town near the modern railway station in 1885, some inscribed FIR, presumably for *Firmani* (see below),[7] and over 160 bullets found west of the town in 1985, perhaps at the besiegers' encampment.[8] In 1990 Thomas Völling was able to examine 1283 bullets

---

[1] Gabba 1994; Dart 2014; Santangelo 2017.
[2] Laffi and Pasquinucci 1975: 20.
[3] Zangemeister 1885: 5-47, repeated with minor alterations from his entries in *CIL* IX (1883): pp. 631-47 at no. 6086.
[4] Gabrielli and Zangemeister 1877; Zangemeister 1885: 5; Laffi and Pasquinucci 1975: 85.
[5] Zangemeister 1885: 5.
[6] Zangemeister 1885: 88; Laffi 1981; Polita 2007: 15.
[7] Gabrielli 1885; Laffi and Pasquinucci 1975: 119.
[8] *Fasti Archaeologici* 1981-82: 437 no. 5667. An intact circular kiln found just outside the 'Porta Gemina' c.

Figure 8. Asculum (Ascoli Piceno, Italy). Course of the Castellano tributary at the Ponte di Cecco. The bridge, of Roman Republican or Augustan date, was reconstructed in the 1960s following wartime demolition. Photo: Pampuco. Wikimedia Commons. Licence: CC BY-SA 4.0.

found at Asculum, and identified six different Types.[9] Those preserved in the Museo Archeologico Statale at Ascoli have been assessed by Elisa Polita,[10] and those at the Museo Nazionale Romano in Rome by Lucio Benedetti.[11]

1825 was initially thought to have been for the manufacture of bullets; but its date and purpose remain unclear (see Zangemeister 1885: 6).
[9] Völling 1990: 52 no. 102.
[10] Polita 2007.
[11] Benedetti 2012b: 375-86 nos VI, 57f-57l.

The Social War and the siege of Asculum, 90-89 BC

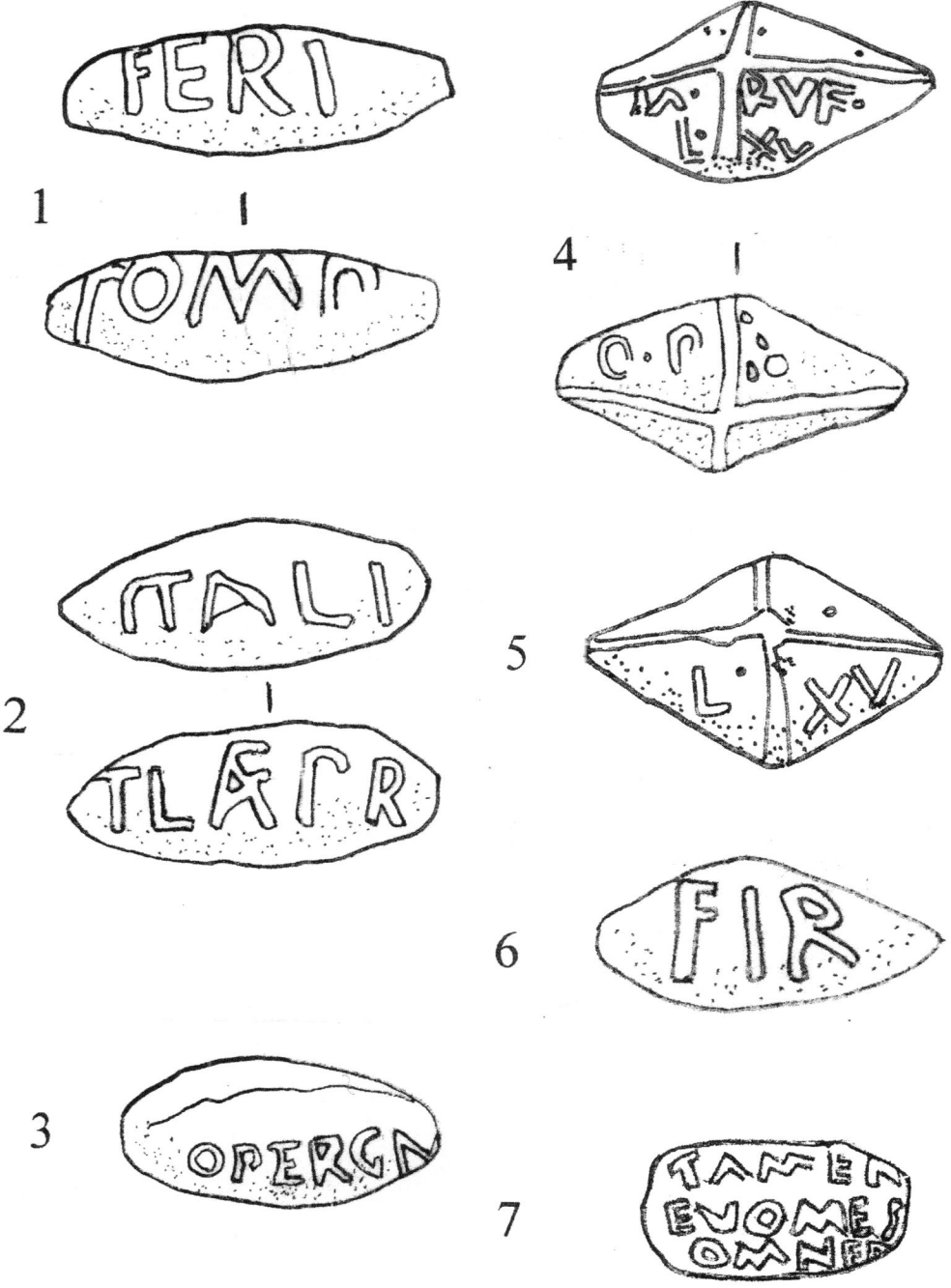

Figure 9. Lead sling bullets from Asculum and vicinity, 90-89 BC. After Zangemeister.
Scale 1:1

A number of individual legions are reported: IX, XI and XV at Asculum itself (Figure 9.4),[12] IIII near Firmum.[13] These are the earliest legions to be individually named on sling bullets. A Marcus Ruf ... is named as belonging to legion XV, but his rank is unspecified (Figure 9.4).[14] Both sides used Latin on their bullets. (For an exception see below).

The Roman legions were supported in the lengthy siege by allied contingents including the *Firmani*, presumably from the adjacent Latin colony of Firmum,[15] which had remained loyal to Rome (Figure 9.6). Another named grouping of soldiers came from the town of Opitergium (Oderzo) in the Veneto, east of Venice,[16] named as *Opitergini* (Figure 9.3) On one bullet (out of about fifteen surviving) the word *Opitergini* is written in Venetic script.[17] Whether these contingents consisted partly or wholly of slingers is not known. Gauls and Spaniards were also present.[18] In later decades only legions are named on sling bullets.

The defenders at Asculum were essentially the local population, supplemented by survivors from nearby battles. Bullets with the inscriptions ITALI and ITALIENSES (as the rebels collectively termed themselves) were manifestly shot outwards by the defenders (Figure 9.2).[19] A considerable number inscribed FERI·POMP, 'Strike Pomp(eius)' (Figure 9.1),[20] were clearly shot against the attackers at a time when Pompeius Strabo commanded the Roman forces conducting the siege. We know from Plutarch that the exhortation *feri* ('Strike') was favoured by Roman soldiers when in pursuit of a fleeing enemy (see also below p. 49).[21] Another bullet reads FER·SAL·POM·FER, understood as *fer sal(utem) Pom(peio) fer.* 'Give Pompeius my greetings', intended sarcastically.[22]

A number of bullets bear personal messages, some shot into the town, others out. One reads ASC[V]LANIS·[D]ON(VM), 'A gift to the people of Asculum'.[23] Another, EM·TIBE·MALVM·MALO, 'Evil upon you, you evil man'.[24] And another, [T]AVRVM / VO[RE]S / MALO / TA[M]EN ·EVOMES·OMNEM, 'I prefer you wolf down bull, but you

---

[12] Zangemeister 1885: nos 24-26; *ILLRP* 1097-98; Benedetti 2012b: nos VI, 57j, 57k, 57l.
[13] Zangemeister 1885: no. 19 = *ILLRP* 1096.
[14] Zangemeister 1885: no. 22 = *ILLRP* 1098. The meaning of the lettering on the reverse side of the bullet is obscure.
[15] Zangemeister 1885: nos 6-8 = *ILLRP* 1091; Benedetti 2012b: no. VI, 57h.
[16] Zangemeister 1885: nos 30-31 = *ILLRP* 1102; Benedetti 2012b: no. VI, 57f.
[17] Zangemeister 1885: no. 45 = Benedetti 2012b: no. VI, 57d. Notice also Zangemeister 1885: no. 32.
[18] Zangemeister 1885: nos 16-17 = *ILLRP* 1095; Benedetti 2012b: no. VI, 57i.
[19] Zangemeister 1885: nos 3-5 = *ILLRP* 1090.
[20] Zangemeister 1885: no. 9 = *ILLRP* 1092. See also Pritchett 1991: 44.
[21] Plut. *Marc.* 8.4. At the battle of Munda in 45 BC (below, p. 44), both sides raised the cry '*Feri*' (Dio 43.37). Bullets at Asculum reading FERI·PICA or, in one case, FERI·PICAM, could allude to the *Picentes*, the local population (Zangemeister 1885: no. 12).
[22] Zangemeister 1885: no. 10.
[23] Zangemeister 1885: no. 11 = *ILLRP* 1093.
[24] Zangemeister 1885: no. 27 = *ILLRP* 1099.

Figure 10. Row of five slingers on a stone relief at Asculum (Ascoli Piceno, Italy). Museo Archeologico Statale di Ascoli Piceno. Photo: Cast in the Museo della Civiltà Romana, Rome. © Roma, Sovrintendenza Capitolina ai Beni Culturali.

spew it all up' (Figure 9.7);[25] the bull was the emblem of the Italian rebels, as their coins confirm. Another reads VENTRI, presumably 'aimed at your belly'.[26] A bullet reading FVGITIVI·PERISTIS, 'You are already doomed, you runaways', was presumably also shot into the town.[27] The runaways here are supposedly slaves,[28] but a more likely target could have been those who had 'run away' from one of the nearby battles and sought refuge in the town. The meaning of some texts remains uncertain.

Asculum has yielded far more lead bullets than any other site of the Late Republic. In contrast to Perusia in 41 BC (below, p. 53), the findspots of many are recorded thanks to Zangemeister and Gabrielli. What do they tell us about the course of the siege? Assuming that the large numbers found in the bed of the Castellano in 1874-79 (see above) were not dumped en masse after the siege ended, we could suppose a major clash; bullets shot by both sides were recovered.

Sling bullets dating to this time are not confined to Asculum itself. A small number were found at the villages of Corropoli,[29] and Tortoreto,[30] both south-east of Asculum, and another near the Latin Colony of Firmum (Fermo) to its north-east.[31] As the occasion for their loss, we could think of the battle fought by Pompeius Strabo near Firmum against the rebel commander Titus Lafrenius,[32] who is named on a surviving bullet from Corropoli (Figure 9.2) as T LAF PR (Titus Lafrenius, *praetor*);[33] his political allegiance is confirmed by ITALI on the bullet's other side.

---

[25] Zangemeister 1885: no. 29 = *ILLRP* 1100. Cf. Zangemeister 1885: no. 28 = *ILLRP* 1101.
[26] Zangemeister 1885: no. 34.
[27] Zangemeister 1885: no. 13 = *ILLRP* 1094.
[28] Rothenhöfer 2018.
[29] Zangemeister 1885: no. 3 = *ILLRP* 1089-90.
[30] Zangemeister 1885: no. 6 = *ILLRP* 1091.
[31] Zangemeister 1885: no. 19 = *ILLRP* 1096.
[32] App. *BC* 1.40, 47.
[33] Zangemeister 1885: no. 3 = *ILLRP* 1089. Lafrenius was *praetor* of the Italian rebels.

A limestone relief, now in the Museo Archeologico Statale at Ascoli, depicts a line of five slingers in slightly different poses (Figure 10).[34] They are tunic-clad and naked above the waist. Each (with the exception of the left-hand figure whose right arm is broken away) carries a sling in his right hand and in his left hand perhaps a bag or sack containing his supply of bullets. The figure on the right is whirling his sling in preparation for casting. The depiction of five figures suggests slingers drawn up in line for a battle, but whether this panel is from a tomb or a commemorative monument is unknown. It is tempting to associate it with the siege of 90-89 BC, or the associated battles nearby. Whether their bullets were of stone, clay or lead cannot be determined.

---

[34] Völling 1990: 30 Abbildung 10; Raggi 2014: 99. The background looks to have been painted in red.

Figure 11. Silver *denarius* depicting L. Cornelius Sulla, issued in 54 BC by his grandson. The coin legend reads: SVLLA·COS (Sulla consul). Photo: © The Hunterian, University of Glasgow (GLAHM 22407).

Chapter 3

Sulla, Sertorius and Caesar, 89-50 BC

At Pompeii, over 200 uninscribed bullets dating from the siege, otherwise poorly documented, by a Roman army under L. Cornelius Sulla in 89 BC during the Social War have been recovered during excavation, immediately inside the town's walls adjacent to the Herculaneum Gate, where bullets aimed at the defenders overshot their mark (Figure 12).[1] Stone *ballista* balls were also found. Some of the lead bullets had been gathered up at the end of the siege. Large indentations in the walls were evidently caused by *ballista* balls.[2] Small indentations have been claimed as made by sling bullets, but the recent experiments by Dr J.H. Reid have not supported such a view. Clearly slingers were present in Sulla's army, but their identity is not known.[3] Some 50,000 clay bullets, by far the largest cache known, found at the Latin Colony of Paestum in Southern Italy, could belong at this time; perhaps they were prepared in case of an attack but never used.[4]

When Cornelius Sulla was besieging Athens in 87-86 BC, two slaves trapped inside the Roman lines sent details of the defenders' plans to the besiegers, 'written on oval lead bullets'.[5] The slaves kept sending these and similar messages over till they got noticed and came to the attention of the Roman commander. The besieged made a sally, casting stones, javelins and lead bullets. The attackers in their turn bagged up quantities of heavy lead bullets and discharged them from catapults.[6] A few bullets have been found inside the town, some emblazoned with lightning-bolts.[7]

Quintus Sertorius

The activities in Spain between 82 and 72 BC of the renegade Q. Sertorius have attracted renewed interest in recent years. Lead bullets, bearing Sertorius' name in the form Q·SERTOR (with variants in the abbreviation) on one side and often a political watchword on the other, are now known in some quantity (Figure 13.1).[8]

---

[1] Burns 2004; his figures 2-3 usefully show the distribution of bullets and where destruction occurred. For the archaeological context, see Jones and Robinson 2004: 114.
[2] Russo and Russo 2008.
[3] For a bullet reported long ago at Pompeii, see Zangemeister 1885: p. xxiii no. 17 = Volling 1990: 54 no. 126.
[4] Greco and Theodorescu 1980: 17 figura 19.
[5] App. *Mith.* 31. These messages were presumably incised on the bullets after firing rather than inscribed on moulds.
[6] App. *Mith.* 34.
[7] Parsons 1943: 241 figure 26.
[8] Gómez Pantoja and Morales Hernández 2002; Díaz Ariño 2008: 244 nos G2-10; Morillo and Santa Sellés 2019; Noguera *et al.* 2022. Pérez Gutiérrez 2014 usefully assembles the epigraphic, archaeological and numismatic evidence for Sertorius in Spain.

Figure 12. Pompeii, The Anglo-American Project. Excavation in progress close to the Herculaneum Gate, 2004. Photo: © The late Margaret J. Robb. Courtesy of Dr R.F.J. Jones.

The watchwords proclaim his guiding principles: FIDES (Trustworthiness), VERITAS (Integrity), PIETAS (Loyalty) and IVS (Justice),[9] wording presumably determined by Sertorius himself. Many bullets give him the title *proco(n)s(ul)* which he either held legitimately or had assumed for himself in Spain.[10] The bullets can also carry symbols: *fasces* (signifying a legitimate Roman magistrate's authority), a rudder, an anchor and a palm frond. The rudder and anchor could suggest naval activity;[11] the palm denotes a victory. Sertorius' army clearly included slingers, but we do not know their ethnic origins; perhaps they were Balearic, or local Hispanic. His Roman opponents, the proconsuls Q. Caecilius Metellus Pius and Pompey the Great, had slingers too (see below).

Sertorius proved a consummate political operator and master tactician, defeating a succession of generals sent from Rome against him and attracting to his side

---

[9] Beltrán Lloris 1990.
[10] Garcia González 2019 discusses his rank and status.
[11] For which see Plut. *Sert.* 6.2, 7.4. A different interpretation is preferred by Díaz Ariño 2005: 227; 2008: 247.

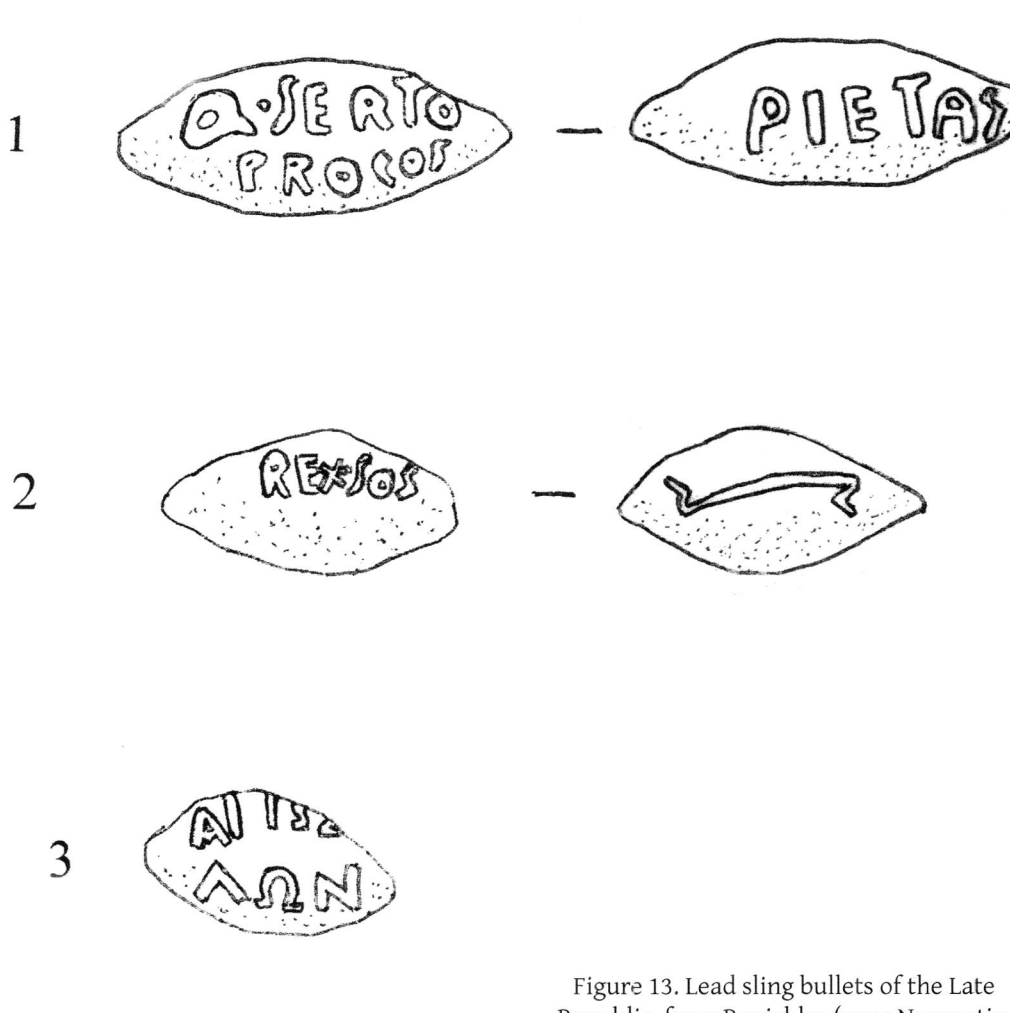

Figure 13. Lead sling bullets of the Late Republic, from Renieblas (near Numantia, Spain), naming Quintus Sertorius (no. 1); Volubilis (Morocco), naming Sosus, King of Mauretania; the other side shows what may be a stylised lightning-bolt (no. 2); Numantia (Spain), recording in Greek the Aetolian slingers (no. 3); Apsorus (Croatia), from a suggested siege (no. 4). After Gómez Pantoja and Morales Hernández (nos 1, 3), Roma Numismatics Limited (no. 2), Zangemeister (no. 4). Scale 1:1.

many Spanish tribes. The geographical spread of his bullets has been enlarged by their identification at an increasing number of locations, many in the Lower Ebro Valley, others on the east coast of Spain between Valentia (Valencia) and Carthago Nova (Cartagena), and others again further to the south and west.[12] They also help to establish his routes of march.[13]

Excavation of the one-legion winter fortress at Cáceres el Viejo north of Mérida, which suffered destruction at around this time, yielded numerous stone *ballista* balls, found in a store, and at least one clay bullet.[14] Occupation of the small Roman town of La Caridad at Caminreal south of the River Ebro, which is best known for the discovery of an intact torsion catapult found on the floor of a house,[15] similarly ended in destruction, perhaps after a siege.[16] A number of uninscribed lead bullets were recovered at a house in the town's 'Insula 1'; presumably they had been prepared by the town's defenders.[17] As some bullets were fused together, they could not have been shot in active warfare and may therefore have been discarded after manufacturing.

The sieges in 74 and 72 BC by Pompey the Great of the Sertorian stronghold of Calagurris (Calahorra) in the Ebro Valley are illuminated by the discovery of over 300 stone *ballista* balls,[18] which from the findspot belonged to the attackers. One was inscribed CASTRA·MARTIA ('Mars' Camp');[19] *Castra Martia* could be the unlocated headquarters of the besieging force. Another was directed against the Sertorian supporter Marcus Lepidus, despite his having died some years previously; perhaps his one-time soldiers were being targeted.[20] Other balls bore Roman numerals, of uncertain significance.[21]

Excavation of a 'military camp' at Lomba do Canho in the Arganil region of Portugal, north-east of Lisbon, which has been associated with Sertorius, yielded nine uninscribed lead bullets and six heavy stone bullets.[22] Les Tres Cales, on Spain's east coast, has produced 58 lead bullets, of which two were inscribed with Sertorius' name and one of his watchwords, along with much military equipment.[23]

---

[12] Díaz Ariño 2005: 224 with nos 4-24; Pérez Gutiérrez 2014 with figura 32; Morillo and Sala-Sellés 2019 with their figura 4.3; Noguera *et al*. 2022 with their figura 10.
[13] Garcia González 2017.
[14] Ulbert 1984: 111 Tafel 40 no 462.
[15] Vicente *et al*. 1997: 168; Bishop and Coulston 2006: 58; Wilkins 2017: 46.
[16] Morillo and Sala-Sellés 2019: 61; Noguera *et al*. 2022: 20.
[17] Vicente *et al*. 1997: 195 figure 39, 46.
[18] Velaza Frías *et al*. 2003.
[19] *AE* 2003, 969a; Díaz Ariño 2008: 257 no. PC2.
[20] *AE* 2003, 969b. Díaz Ariño 2008: 257 no. PC1. The inscription reads: EXER[..]TO·EEIV·FVGA·M·LEP[I]D, with the word FORMIDINE added. The words *exercitus* (army), *fuga* (flight), and *formido* (fear) feature in this puzzling text. A legion IV may also be mentioned.
[21] Díaz Ariño 2008: 259 nos PC 3-29. For inscribed *ballista* balls at Urso (Osuna), see below p. 44.
[22] Guerra 1987; De Castro Nunes, Fabião and Guerra 1988: 14 figura 9; Morillo and Aurrecoechea 2006: 115, 168.
[23] Noguera *et al*. 2022: 14.

Figure 14. France, Belgium, Holland, Germany (Roman Gaul), showing places mentioned in the text.

The activities of his eventually victorious opponents have also become better known. To be associated with them are about 2000 lead bullets found on a hillside at Azuaga, Badajoz province, together with lead slag suggesting a manufacturing site.[24] Some of the bullets were inscribed Q ME (or variants) for Q. Caecilius Metellus Pius.[25] We know from Plutarch that Metellus Pius in Spain had at his disposal 2000 slingers and archers;[26] they were deployed in an attack on an unnamed walled town, presumably

---

[24] Domergue 1970: figures 3-4; Díaz Ariño 2008: 243 no. G1. What percentage of the total bore inscriptions is unclear.
[25] *AE* 1993, 1015 = Díaz Ariño 2005: 224 with nos 1-3; 2008: 243 no. G1. Two are held in the Museo Archeológico de Sevilla (Fernández Gómez 2009: 152 nos 31-32).
[26] Plut. *Sert.*12.

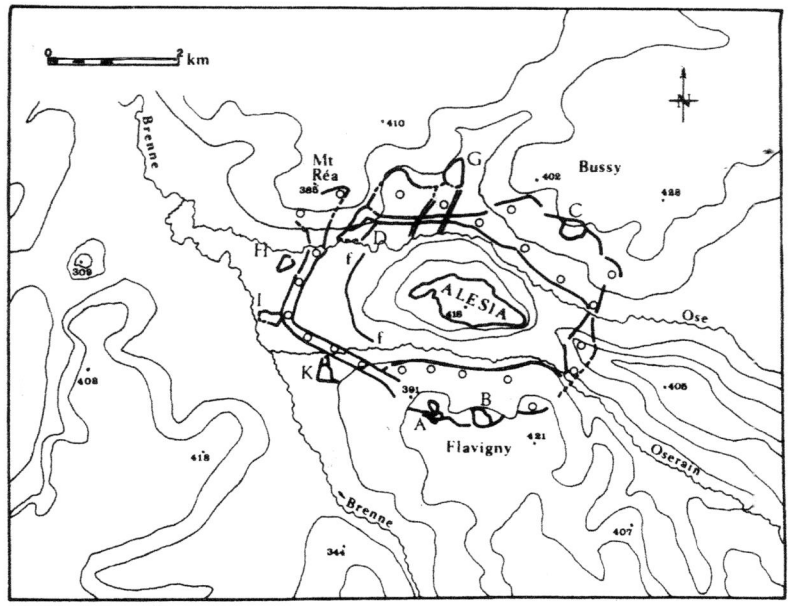

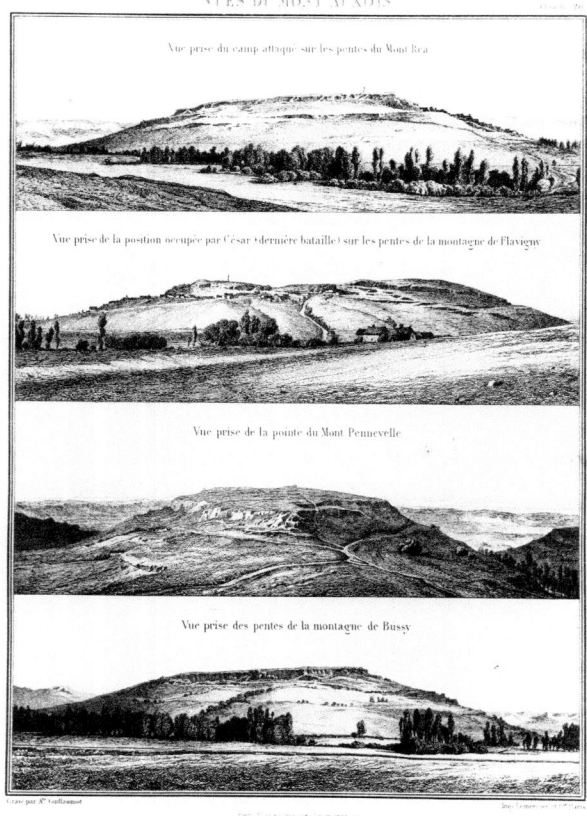

Figure 15. Alesia (Alise-Sainte-Reine, France). 1. Site-plan. After L. Keppie, *The Making of the Roman Army*, 1984, London: figure 28. 2. Views of the hill in the 19th century. After Napoléon III, *Historie de Jules Céscr*, Paris, 1865-70: planche 26.

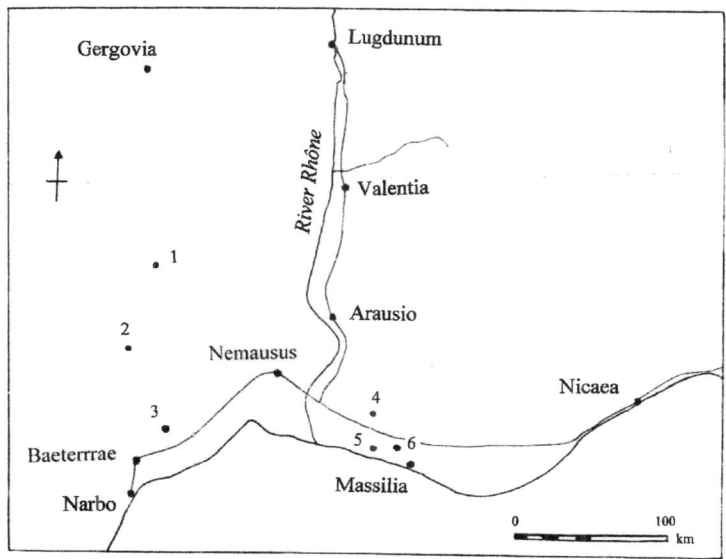

Figure 16. South of France, showing places mentioned in the text.
Note: 1. Altès; 2. Saint-Affrique; 3. Saint-Pargoire; 4. Les Petites Caisses; 5. Saint-Blaise; 6. La Cloche.

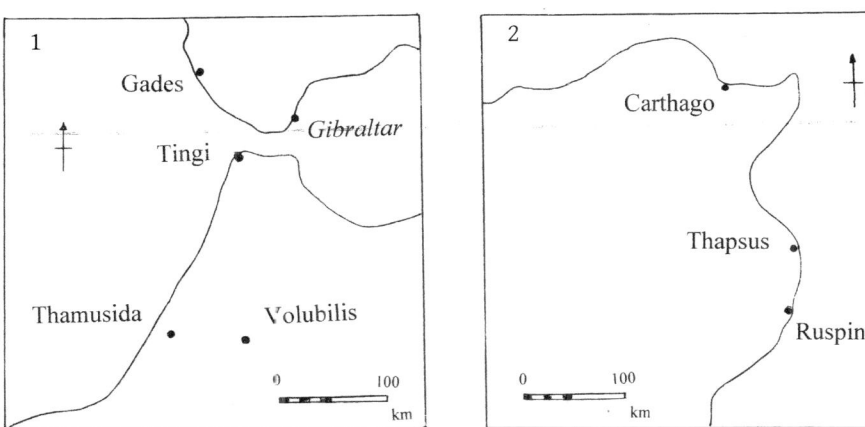

Figure 17. North Africa, showing places mentioned in the text.
1. Mauretania.
2. Numidia.

held by supporters of Sertorius.[27] The murder of Sertorius in 72 BC by his deputy, M. Perperna, effectively brought the insurgency to an end.

At the hilltop site of Botromagno (Silvium), Gravina di Puglia, Southern Italy, 225 lead sling bullets were found by metal detecting, which, it is suggested, could testify to an assault by the forces of Spartacus in 73-71 BC.[28] Some bullets bore single Latin letters.[29]

Many eastern campaigns were undertaken by the Roman army at this time, down to the great defeat suffered by M. Licinius Crassus at Carrhae in 53 BC. It is scarcely to be doubted that slingers served in them, but we know only that L. Licinius Lucullus deployed slingers in his attack on the Armenian capital, Tigranocerta in 69 BC.[30] The campaign conducted in Crete by Q. Caecilius Metellus (*Creticus*) in 63 BC is illustrated by a single bullet found near the town of Rhithymna (Rethymno), bearing the letters ME.[31]

Caesar in Gaul, 58-50 BC

Caesar's campaigns involved many battles and assaults on native strongholds.[32] His legions grew in number from four to 10;[33] they were supported in 57 BC by Balearic slingers, Numidian and Cretan archers, and light cavalry.[34] Coins of the Balearic Island of Ibiza in found in Gaul could form a guide to the location of their activities under Caesar.[35] Later references to slingers in his army do not specify their ethnic origins. They were deployed on campaign when light-armed forces were called for, in place of the heavily armed legionaries.[36] Lead bullets have been found near Bibracte (Mont Beuvray, Burgundy),[37] and at Gergovia (Gergovie, Clermont-Ferrand),[38] both scenes of intense fighting at this time. Some 30 lead bullets, none bearing inscriptions, are reported on a plateau near the town of Thuin (Hainaut, Belgium),[39] which is suggested as the stronghold of the Atuatuci, besieged by Caesar in 57 BC; but the identification is

---

[27] Aul. Gell. *Noct. Att.* 9.1.1.
[28] Schinco and Small 2020; Small and Small 2022: 185. See also Rothenhöfer 2018.
[29] Schinco and Small 2020: 99.
[30] Plut. *Luc.* 27.2
[31] Guarducci 1939: xxiv no. 24; Kelly 2012: 285 fig. 8.
[32] Poux (2008: 365-71) provides a wide-ranging assessment of sling bullets at the time of the Gallic War. (Poux 2000 is a preliminary survey of the evidence). For uninscribed lead bullets found in Roman camps at Lautagne on the River Rhône near Valentia (Valence), possibly dating to this time, see Feugère *et al.* 2020: 335.
[33] Brunt 1971: 466.
[34] Caes. *BG* 2.7.
[35] Reddé 2019: 94. For a different interpretation, see Doyen 2011.
[36] Caes. *BG* 2.10, 19, 24, 8.40.
[37] Pernet *et al.* 2008: 105 nos 42-51.
[38] Poux *et al.* 2008 figure 7.16; Reddé 2019: 94 figure 6.5.
[39] Roymans and Fernández-Götz 2015; Roymans 2019: 115 with figure 7.1.

disputed.[40] There were slingers on board Caesar's warships when he landed in Britain in 55 BC.[41] Surprisingly perhaps, Caesar fails to mention archers or slingers as present in his much larger expeditionary force in 54.[42] The siege of the hilltop stronghold of Alesia (Alise-Sainte-Reine, Burgundy) in 52 BC was the climax of the war (Figure 15).[43] There were slingers active on both sides.[44] The site has yielded at least 29 lead sling bullets, mostly from surface survey in the 1990s.[45] There are three distinct shapes.[46] Two of the bullets name Caesar's trusted legate Titus Labienus, in the form T·LABI (Figure 18.2).[47] Two bullets from the nineteenth-century excavations at the site also carried inscriptions: the first read HAT; the other bore five or six letters, perhaps BRI·PIS (Figures 18.3-4).[48] Sievers suggested slingers from the town of Hatria (Atri), near Teramo, Italy, and from either Pisaurum (Pesaro) or Picenum,[49] but the abbreviated names of officers in Caesar's army are more likely. One bullet carries a lightning-bolt emblem.[50] No legions are individually named on the surviving bullets at Alesia. There seems no record of any clay bullets, as used by the Gauls, being found there. An undated bullet found in Paris during excavations on Montagne Sainte-Geneviève (Figure 18.1) reads VIXI, apparently 'I have lived' (or 'My life is over').[51]

Lead bullets have been reported at several other locations in Southern France, but many are datable to earlier periods.[52] They include hillforts at Petites Caisses de Mouriès, east of Arles,[53] and at Saint-Affrique south-west of Millau (Figure 16).[54] Excavation of a promontory site at Saint-Blaise north-west of Marseille yielded stone *ballista* balls and sling bullets of stone, clay and lead.[55] A bullet from Altès (Sévérac-le-Château), north of Millau, appears to read MALRIP, with at least two letters reversed.[56] We could think here of L. Manlius, *proconsul* of Transalpine Gaul in 78 BC.[57] A bullet

---

[40] Paridaens *et al.* 2020.
[41] Caes. *BG* 4.25.
[42] Polyaenus, writing in the second century AD, reports that Caesar brought an elephant to Britain, equipped with a 'tower' in which archers and slingers were placed (*Strat.* 8.23.5). However, the story belongs better under Claudius (see Scullard 1974: 194 with Dio 60.21).
[43] Caes. *BG* 7.68-88. See now Le Bohec 2021:157.
[44] Caes. *BG* 7.81. A lead ingot and lead offcuts are also reported (Deyber 1994: 268 at no. 213), as are stone *ballista* balls (Deyber 1994: 268 no. 214; Sievers 2001: 173).
[45] Sievers 2001: planche 84 nos 724-52; Sievers 2007.
[46] Brouquier-Reddé 1997: 280 figure 3.
[47] *AE* 1995, 1094a and 1094b, found during surface survey over Camp C (Sievers 1996: 77; Sievers 2001: planche 84 nos 726-27). Labienus is also named on a bullet found at Agedincum (Sens), north-west of Alesia (Zangemeister 1885: no. 963*).
[48] Sievers 1996: 76; Sievers 2001: planche 84 nos 724-25.
[49] Sievers 2007: 248.
[50] Feugère 2002:160.
[51] Poux and Robin 2000: 210 figure 18.2; Poux 2008: 371 figure 46.
[52] On bullets recovered during fieldwork at the battlefield of Arausio (Orange), 105 BC, see Deyber and Luginbühl 2018: 158, 161.
[53] Marcadal *et al.* 2017.
[54] Gruat *et al.* 2002.
[55] Rolland 1951: 135 with figures 159-60.
[56] Gruat 2006: 113 with figures 1-2.
[57] Alternatively, the inscription could report M. Agrippa (on whom see below p. 64).

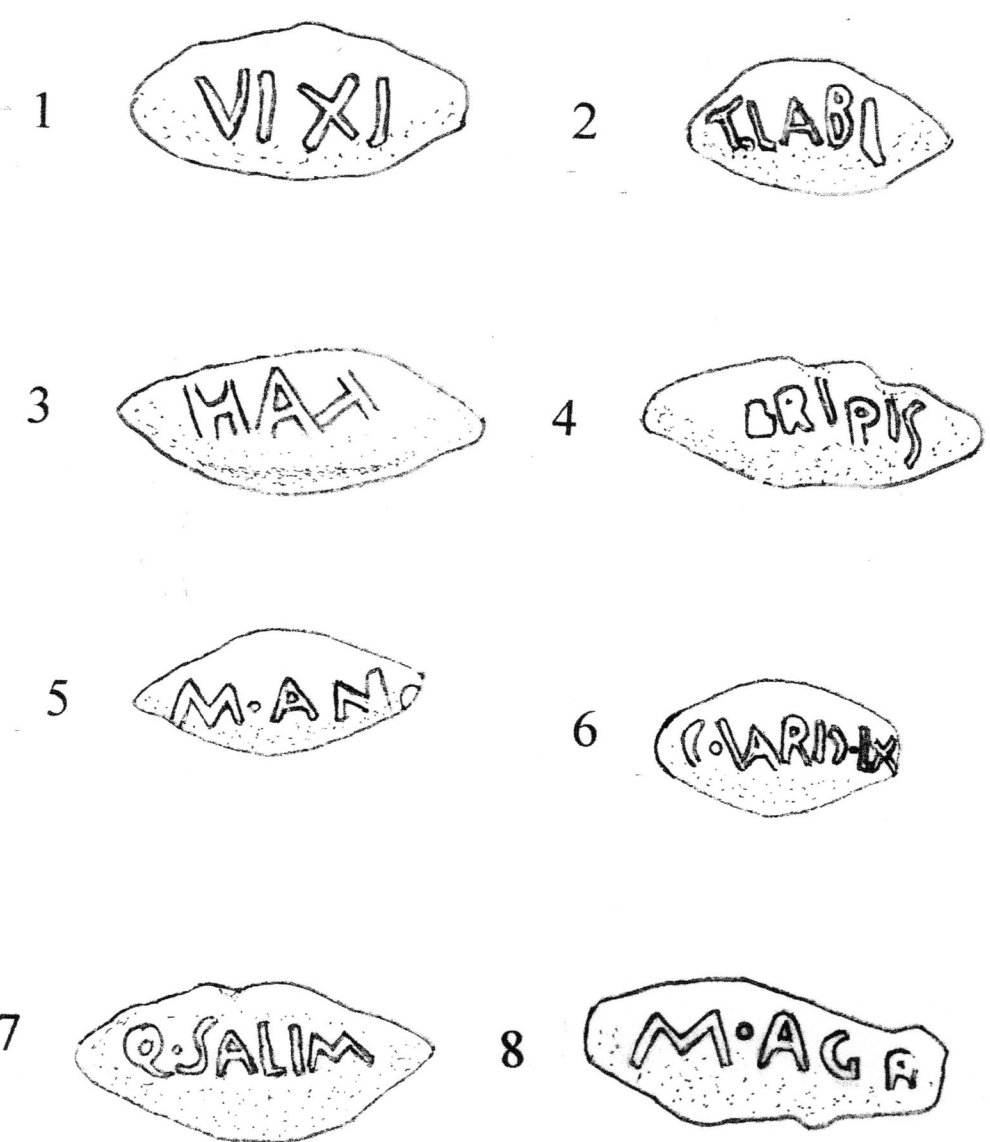

Figure 18. Lead sling bullets of the Late Republic, from Paris (no. 1), Alesia (nos 2-4), Le Mas d'Agenais (no. 5), Saint-Pargoire (no. 6), Sicily (no. 7), L'Ermitage d'Agen (no. 8). After Poux and Robin (no. 1), Sievers (nos 2-4), Feugère (nos 5-6), Costabile (no. 7), Verdin (no. 8). Scale 1:1.

from Le Mas d'Agenais (near Agen) in Southern France, inscribed M·AN, may also report L. Manlius (Figure 18.5).[58] Alternatively it could record Mark Antony (Marcus Antonius) who served as a legate under Caesar in Gaul between 52 and 50 BC;[59] another bullet with the same inscription has been found in Palestine.[60]

Sosus, King of Mauretania.

Two groups of lead bullets from the client kingdom of Mauretania (partly modern Morocco, partly western Algeria) shed an unexpected light (Figure 17.1). Firstly, a group of six inscribed REX·SOS, found together at Volubilis, south of Tingi (Tangier),[61] name King Sosus (Figure 13.2), about whom almost nothing is known, except that he reigned sometime between 80 and 49 BC.[62] This is the only known instance of a client king following the Roman practice of having lead bullets inscribed in Latin with his name. The circumstances of their manufacture remain unknown, as does the identity of the slingers who were presumably mercenaries in the service of the king. The bullets were found in a wadi beside the 'Temple B (the 'Temple of Saturn').[63] We have to assume a conflict, real or anticipated, at some point in the civil war period, but we cannot say who the King's adversaries were. A group of 29 mainly inscribed lead bullets from the nearby town of Thamusida (Sidi Ali ben Ahmed) bear the inscription R·E·F, which has been tentatively expanded as R(EX·BOCCHVS)·E(T·SOSI)·F ('Bocchus, king and son of Sosus').[64] The emblem on the reverse of many of the bullets at both sites is clearly delineated on an example recently advertised for sale on the internet.[65] It is suggested as a stylised lightning-bolt,[66] but does not resemble the bolts depicted on many bullets of this period (e.g. Figures 32.1, 32.3).

---

[58] Feugère 2002: 160 figure 216.
[59] Verdin 2013: 95 figure 21. On bullets found at Mutina and at Perusia (below, pp. 49, 54), Mark Antony's name is abbreviated to M·ANT, M·ANTO and M·ANTON.
[60] Stiebel 1997: 303.
[61] Chatelain 1942; AE 1942/43, 53; Marion 1960: 488 with planche xvi; Völling 1990: 50 no.74.
[62] Coins of his likely successor, King Bocchus II, describe him as SOSI F ('son of Sosus').
[63] Marion 1960: 488.
[64] Callu et al. 1965: 104. It is hard to find a convincing expansion, except that R should be the abbreviation for REX and F could be FECIT ('made'). No suitable regal name is attested.
[65] Roma Numismatics Limited, E-sale 74 (20 August 2020), Lot 1506.
[66] Callu et al. 1965: 104.

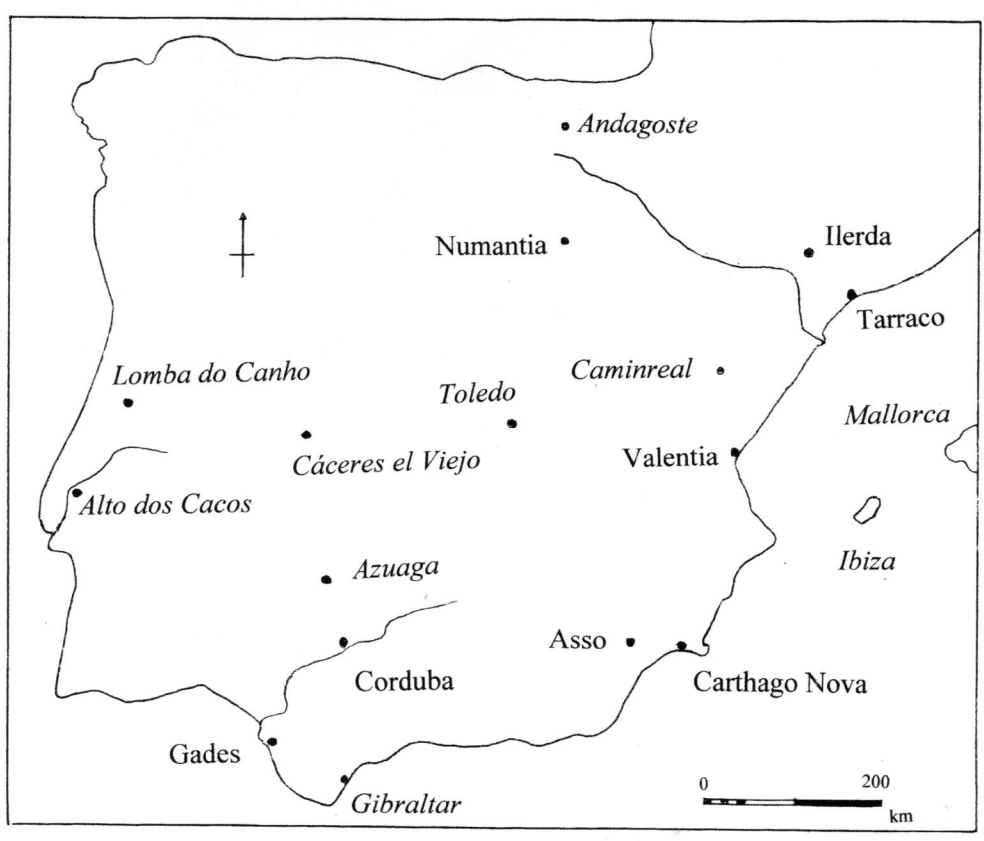

Figure 19. Spain and Portugal, showing places mentioned in the text

Chapter 4

Civil war 1: Caesar against Pompey and his sons, 49-45 BC

Caesar's crossing in January 49 of the River Rubicon, the boundary between his province of Cisalpine Gaul and Italy, precipitated civil war with Pompey and his many supporters. Pompey himself quickly withdrew from Italy eastwards across the Adriatic (below p. 40). Archers and slingers formed his rearguard at Brundisium (Brindisi);[1] their ethnicity is not reported.

Caesar did not pursue him at once, but moved westwards into Spain, where Pompey's legates Lucius Afranius and Marcus Petreius commanded six legions.[2] An attack on a settlement at La Cloche near Massilia (Marseille) is likely to belong in 49 BC (Figure 16), at a time when Caesar's troops were laying siege to Marseille itself; excavation has yielded uninscribed sling bullets.[3] Along Caesar's route into Spain lay the site at Puig Ciutat ('Hill City') which seems to have been violently destroyed at this time, perhaps after resistance from Pompeian defenders (Figure 21). A number of uninscribed sling bullets were among the finds, as well as iron catapult bolt-heads.[4]

The poet Lucan's *Pharsalia*, composed about a century after the event, features an incident from a naval battle off Marseille in 49 BC, in which a Balearic slinger named as Lygdamus (evidently in the employ of the Massiliots) shoots a lead bullet which hits a Roman soldier, named as Tyrrhenus, in the temple, the impact causing both his eyes to pop out of his head.[5] This must surely be testimony to the perceived power of the bullets, but the personal names are likely to be a poetic invention.[6]

The battle of Ilerda, 49 BC

In June 49 BC Caesar defeated Afranius and Petreius at Ilerda (Lleida) in north-east Spain. Battle was joined south of the town. Caesar posted his slingers in the middle of his line.[7] Areas to the south-east of Ilerda have yielded numerous bullets (Figure 21). Of these, 82 all inscribed with the letters SCAE, were found near Picamoixons,

---

[1] Caes. *BC* 1.27.5
[2] A bullet now in the Museo Arqueológico in Seville could, it is suggested here, mention Afranius (Fernández Gómez 2009:151 no. 28).
[3] Chabot and Feugère 1993. Their map shows the distribution of finds, which included a large number of stone *ballista* balls.
[4] Pujol *et al.* 2019: 237 with figure 12.7.
[5] Luc. *Phars.* 3.709-14.
[6] I am advised that the impact of the bullet is unlikely to have resulted in the injury as described.
[7] Caes. *BC.* 1.83.2.

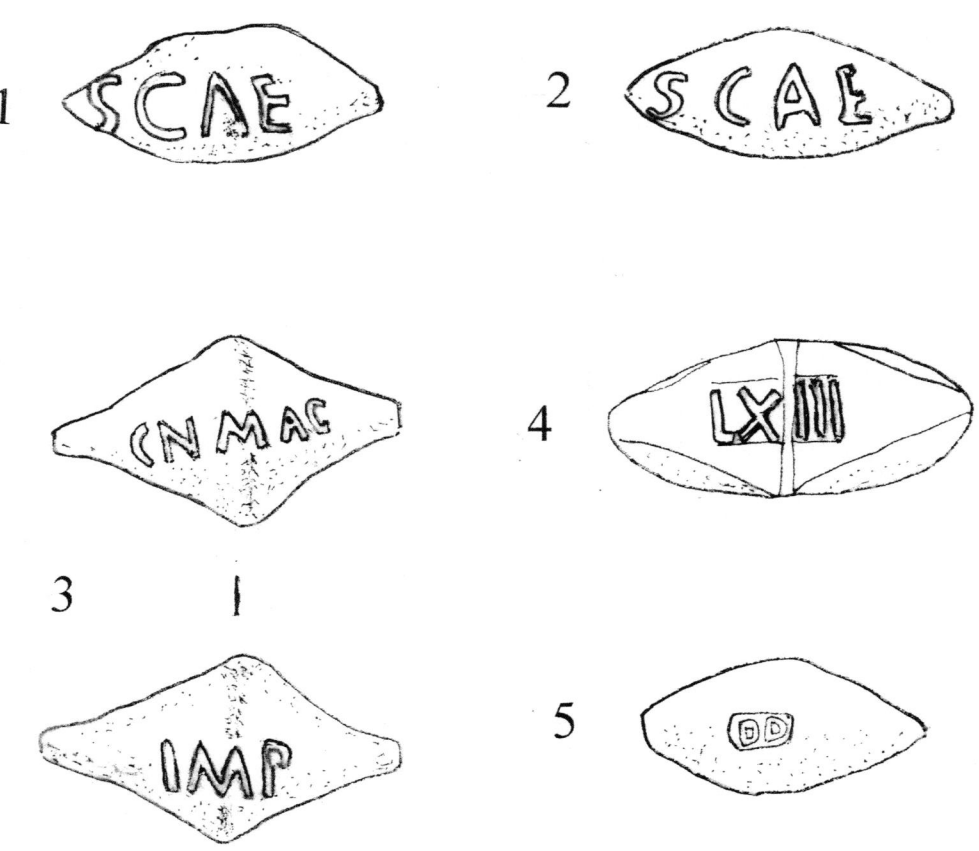

Figure 20. Lead sling bullets, Spain, 49-45 BC, from Ilerda (no. 1), Menorca (no. 2), Urso (no. 3), Cerro de las Balas (nos 4-5). After López Vilar (no. 1), De Nicolàs (no. 2); Díaz Ariňo (no. 3), Pina Polo and Zanier (nos 4-5). Scale 1:1.

nearer to Tarragona (Figure 20.1-2).[8] They were retrieved from a ploughed field, in a radius of 50m, together with coins and pottery; perhaps there had been a camp here or a manufacturing site.[9] A silver denarius of 106 BC and seven undatable small-denomination Gaulish coins were found in association. As three of these were Marseille issues, they could have been brought by Caesarian soldiers who had been present at the siege of Marseille, then in progress.[10]

---

[8] López Vilar 2013a; 2013b; Moralejo Ordax and Saavedra 2016; Noguera *et al.* 2018.
[9] López Vilar 2013b: 432.
[10] López Vilar 2013b: 434 figura 6.

CIVIL WAR 1: CAESAR AGAINST POMPEY AND HIS SONS, 49-45 BC

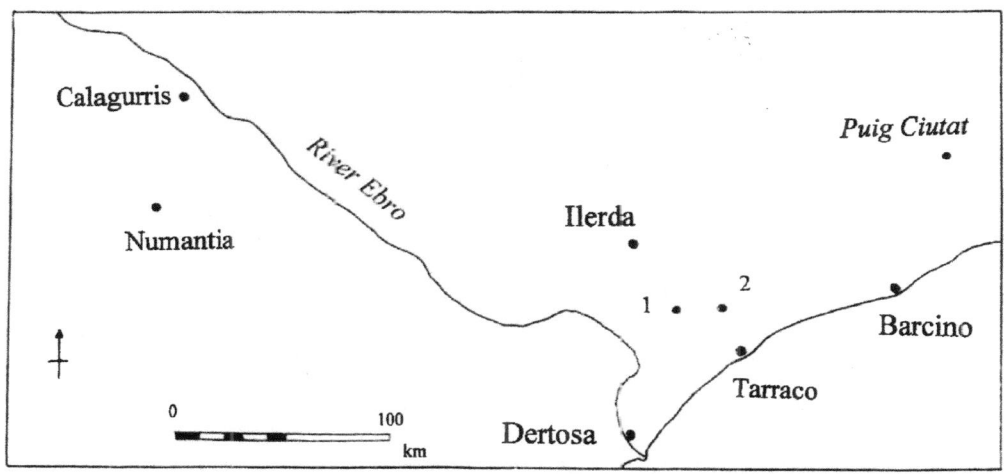

Figure 21. North-Eastern Spain, to illustrate events in 133-49 BC.
Note: 1. Prades; 2. Picamoixons.

Another two bullets were found nearby at Prades, one bearing the same abbreviation SCAE, the other the numerals XII. It has been supposed that this indicates the presence at Ilerda of a legion XII.[11] Caesar's legion XII is not otherwise known to have taken part in the Ilerda campaign; perhaps this was an otherwise unattested Pompeian legion.[12] Two bullets from Dertosa (Tortosa) south of Tarraco (Tarragona) read XII and CN MAG (*Gnaeus Magnus*).[13] The latter could relate to events in 45 BC (below, p. 42). Other examples of the abbreviation SCAE come from Huete near Toledo and from the island of Menorca (Figure 20.2), which count against them being a local phenomenon.[14]

The meaning of SCAE, likely to be an abbreviated Roman name, is disputed. We could think here of Scaeva, Caesar's centurion in legion VI, soon to be commended for his heroism at Dyrrhachium in 48 BC, after which he was promoted to be *primus pilus* of his legion (below p. 41).[15] The name Scaeva recurs on a sling bullet of 41 BC from Perugia (below p. 57; Figure 32.8). However, no military affiliation is indicated here. On some of the bullets the letter S is separated by a gap from CAE (see Figure 20.2); alternatively it has been suggested that we have here reference to a Q(uintus) CAE(cilius), i.e. Q. Caecilius Metellus Pius (on whom see above p. 24), the S being

---

[11] López Vilar 2013b: 435, 438; Noguera *et al.* 2018: 900.
[12] For bullets with the numerals XII in Sicily, see Manganaro 2000: 129 with figure 29-30. An unprovenanced lead bullet reading LEG XII is held at the Museo Arqueológico in Seville (Fernández Gómez 2009: 149 no. 19).
[13] López Vilar 2013b: 437.
[14] Contreras Rodrigo *et al.* 2006: figura 5; Moralejo Ordax and Saavedra 2016: 56; Müller *et al.* 2014: figure 1; Müller 2018: 26.
[15] Moralejo Ordax and Saavedra 2016: 56, 64.

Figure 22. Silver *denarius*, showing an elephant trampling a serpent, 49-48 BC. The coin legend reads: CAESAR. Photo: © The Hunterian, University of Glasgow (GLAHM 22426).

interpreted as a reversed Q.[16] On the other hand, Géza Alföldy made the attractive suggestion that SCAE is abbreviated from Scaevola, the surname of a patrician Roman family, of which a likely descendent, P. Mucius Scaevola, is attested in nearby Tarraco at this time.[17] Alföldy proposed that this Scaevola was serving Caesar in a senior position in 49 BC, perhaps as a legate.

Another possibility could be that the bullets report Sextus Julius Caesar, a young cousin of Gaius Julius Caesar, who served in the Ilerda campaign in an unspecified capacity,[18] perhaps as *tribunus militum* in a legion.[19] In 47 he was *quaestor* at Rome and

---

[16] Díaz Ariño 2008: 255 no. G39. Moralejo Ordax and Saavedra (2016: 56) consider this interpretation very forced.
[17] Alföldy 1975: no. 2. Cf. López Vilar 2013b: 441.
[18] Caes. *BC* 2.20. See Münzer 1918: 477 no. 153.
[19] Broughton 1951: 264. The identification, if accepted, would confirm that these bullets are datable to 49 BC.

Figure 23. Greece, showing places mentioned in the text.

in 46 made governor of Syria with at least one legion.[20] The inscription on the Ilerda bullets could therefore be read as S(extus) CAE(sar),[21] with no interpunct.[22]

Dyrrhachium and Pharsalus, 48 BC

On his return to Rome, Caesar soon eliminated the remaining Pompeian supporters in Italy. Pompey spent the rest of the year, 49 BC, gathering troops from Rome's

---

[20] Brunt 1971: 477 footnote 1.
[21] For CAE as the abbreviation on lead bullets for CAESAR, see Díaz Ariño 2008: 249 no. G14.
[22] For an absence of interpuncts, see Figures 9.2, 13.4, 18.6-7, 20.3-4, 35.

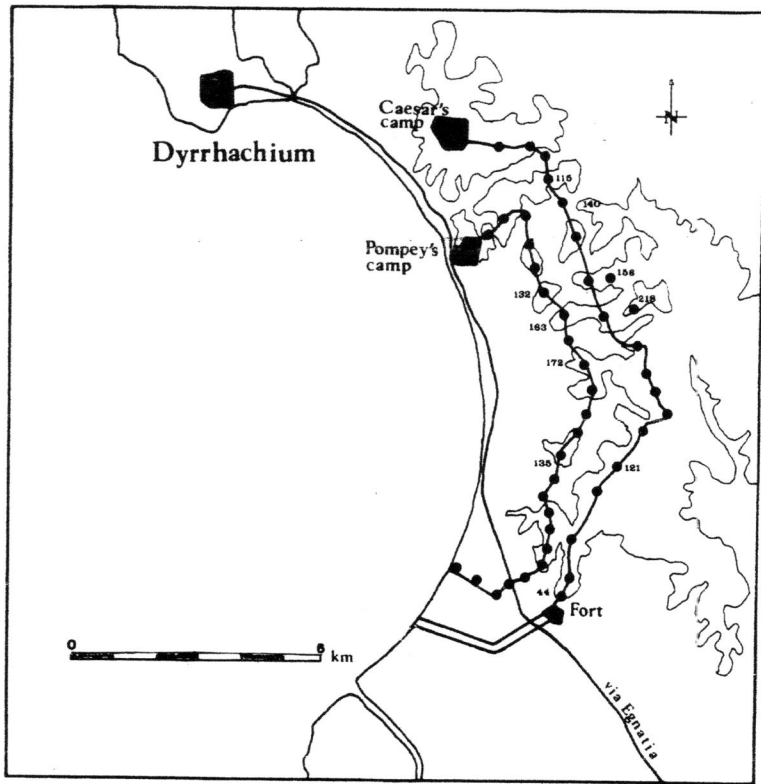

Figure 24. Siegelines constructed by Caesar and by Pompey at Dyrrhachium (Durrës, Albania), 48 BC. The siting of individual forts, marked here by dots, is largely hypothetical. After L. Keppie, *The Making of the Roman Army*, 1984, London: figure 31).

eastern provinces and from client kings. Anticipating an onslaught by Caesar, he concentrated his army at Dyrrhachium (Durrës, Albania) in the Roman province of Macedonia. This was the western starting-point of the *Via Egnatia*, the Roman road which crossed Northern Greece on its way to Thessalonica (Thessaloniki) and Byzantium, later Constantinople (Istanbul).

In January 48 BC Caesar caught Pompey off-guard by swiftly transferring the bulk of his army eastwards across the Adriatic. Caesar brought 11 legions, and Pompey had nine, with another two expected.[23] The following months witnessed the construction by each side of a continuous rampart and ditch over a distance of 15-17 Roman miles (22-25 kms) in the hilly terrain south of Dyrrhachium (Figure 24).[24] Caesar had hoped

---

[23] Brunt 1971: 473.
[24] Veith 1920: 147 with Abbildungen 1-20.

to hem in Pompey's army by what was in effect a circumvallation, and Pompey to prevent him.[25] Numerous forts (*castella*) were built on high points along both lines; some upstanding traces have been observed by fieldwork.[26] Caesar provides a detailed narrative of the confused and intense fighting extending over several months, which saw very substantial forces operating in sometimes closely confined spaces, with heavy losses incurred on both sides.[27]

The slingers in Pompey's army in 49 BC, at the beginning of the campaign, had amounted to two cohorts, each of 600 men.[28] They could equate to the slingers Pompey drew from Crete and from Thrace.[29] At Dyrrhachium, Pompey's slingers and archers directed showers of bullets and arrows against Caesar's soldiers as they were endeavouring to finish his fortifications.[30] Caesar too had slingers, evidently part of his expeditionary force; they were deployed to cover the retreat of the Ninth legion from an exposed position in one of the *castella*.[31] As Pompey's archers proved particularly effective, Caesar's soldiers devised protective clothing against them.[32] Similarly Pompey's legionaries made wicker coverings for their helmets, against stones thrown by the Caesarian troops.[33]

Scaeva, a centurion in the Sixth Legion, was singled out by Caesar for his exploits in defending one of the *castella*, becoming a byword for bravery against impossible odds.[34] Caesar promoted him to *primus pilus* (chief centurion) of his legion, and rewarded him (and the others in his cohort) financially.[35] However, it was Caesar who was worsted in these exchanges and he was eventually forced to give up the attempted blockade, retiring southeastwards into Greece.

The protagonists met again south of Larissa (in Thessaly, Greece), in the vicinity of the town of Pharsalus (Fársala). It proved a decisive victory for Caesar's experienced legions. Slingers were in action on both sides.[36] In the course of the battle, when Pompey's slingers and archers were left exposed by shifts in the battle line, they were

---

[25] Caes. *BC* 3.43-44.
[26] Kromayer and Veith 1922-29: Blatt 20.
[27] Caes. *BC* 3.44, 46, 54, 63. Cf. App. *BC* 2. 60; Dio 41.50. See Goldsworthy 2006: 414; Sheppard 2006: 40; Sampson 2022: 147.
[28] Caes. *BC* 3.4.
[29] App. *BC* 2.49, 71.
[30] Caes. *BC* 3.44.
[31] Caes. *BC* 3.46.
[32] Caes. BC 3.44.
[33] Caes. *BC* 3.63.
[34] The poet Lucan provides a lengthy account of his exploits which terminate (incorrectly) in heroic death from his many wounds (*Phars*. 6.140). See Hömke 2010.
[35] Caes. *BC* 3.53. For Scaeva, see also above p. 37, below p. 57.
[36] Caes. *BC* 3.88, 93, 94; Lucan *Phars*. 7.512; App. *BC* 2.75; Dio 41.59-60.

slaughtered by Caesarian legionaries.[37] The precise location of the battlefield is much debated,[38] and no sling bullets have to my knowledge been recovered.

Campaigns in Africa and Spain, 46-45 BC

The civil war was not brought to a close with Caesar's great victory in Greece. He proceeded to Egypt where he was opposed at Alexandria by the Egyptian army under King Ptolemy XIII, the younger brother of Cleopatra. Egyptian ships on the adjacent River Nile carried contingents of archers and slingers.[39]

On returning to Italy, Caesar was soon required to cross the Mediterranean again, to North Africa (Figure 17.2), where he was engaged by Pompeian forces under Labienus and Petreius. By 3 January 46 he had established himself at Ruspina (near Monastir, Tunisia); he quickly realised how unbalanced his forces were and had archers brought ashore from his ships. No mention is made of slingers. Smithies were set up for the fashioning of arrows and throwing-weapons, and the casting of lead sling bullets. Moreover, he sent to Sicily for more raw materials, specified as iron and lead, the latter presumably to make bullets.[40] This is the only time the manufacturing of sling bullets is reported in a literary source, perhaps because the circumstances were unusual. Caesar's main force of archers and slingers, 1000 strong, arrived a few weeks later in a second convoy, along with two more legions.[41]

Caesar's opponents in Africa practised making their elephants familiar with 'small stones' aimed at them by their own slingers, in anticipation of the battle at Thapsus that was to follow.[42] But to no avail; when battle was joined, the elephants, terrified by the whirring sound of the slings and of the stone and lead being launched against them, wheeled round into friendly ranks.[43]

The focus then shifted to Spain, where Pompey's sons, Gnaeus and Sextus, enjoyed substantial support. Lead bullets inscribed CN·MAG (*Gnaeus Magnus*) or CN·MAG·IMP (*Gnaeus Magnus imperator*), are widespread in Southern Spain (Figure 20.3), including at or near the battlefield at Munda (below, p. 45) and at the towns of Ategua and Urso (see below pp. 44).[44] At first sight, the inscriptions refer to Pompey the Great (Gnaeus Pompeius Magnus) who held a command over Roman troops in Spain in the 70s BC, during the war against Sertorius (see above, p. 24).[45] However, it is clear from their

---

[37] Caes. *BC* 3.94.
[38] Pelling 1973; Morgan 1983; Sheppard 2006.
[39] Caes. *Bell. Alex.* 30.
[40] Caes. *Bell. Afr.* 20.
[41] Caes. *Bell. Afr.* 34.
[42] Caes. *Bell. Afr.* 27.
[43] Caes. *Bell. Afr.* 83.
[44] Díaz Ariño 2005: 234 nos 25-57; 2008: 247 no. G11; Beltrán Lloris 2016. A further example is reported at Volubilis in the client kingdom of Mauretania (Marion 1960: 488 with planche xvi).
[45] So Völling 1990: 35.

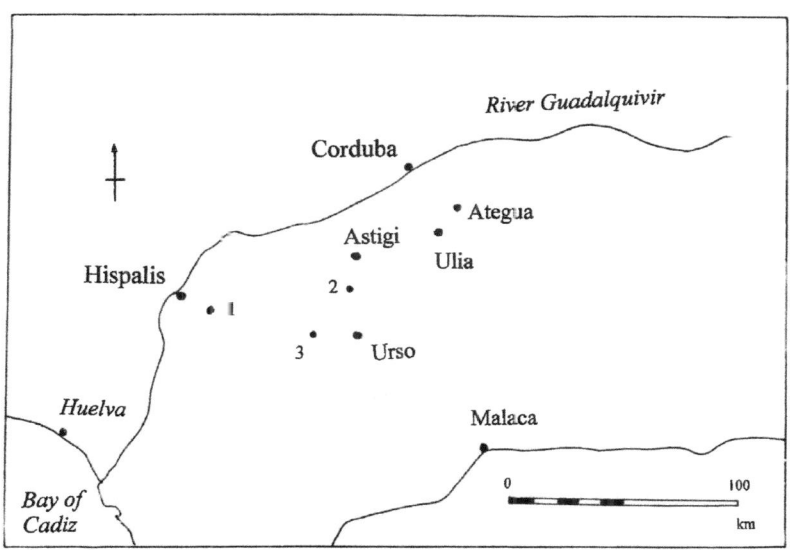

Figure 25. Southern Spain, to illustrate events in 49-45 BC.
Note: 1. Alcalá de Guadaíra; 2. Lantejuela; 3. La Puebla de Cazalla.

distribution that the bullets can be more properly assigned to the period 46-45 BC. when Pompeian troops were under the command of his son, also Gnaeus Pompeius, in association with his younger brother Sextus Pompeius. Both brothers bore the surname *Magnus*, inherited from their father. The younger Gnaeus Pompeius was saluted as *imperator*, as was his brother Sextus, some time in 46-45 BC. The makers of these bullets and their recipients would at once be reminded of the late father; the *nomen* Pompeius was not needed for comprehension.[46]

The town of Irippo (Alcalá de Guadaíra) and its neighbourhood, south-east of Seville (Figure 25), have yielded inscribed bullets, some of which could date to this time. One reads LEG·FIR, presumably *legio firma*, an early example of a legionary title; others bear the letters LEG XIII / Q, and another CA, the latter perhaps a reference to Caesar.[47] The Pompeians in Spain during 46-45 had a legion XIII (see below). Ulia (Montemayor) south of Córdoba suffered two sieges, the first in 47 BC between rival Caesarian factions,[48] the second in 45 BC between Caesar and the Pompeians.[49] Recent excavations have unearthed more than 100 uninscribed sling bullets.[50]

---

[46] No extant bullet in Spain names Sextus Pompeius, but see below p. 62 for bullets in Sicily.
[47] Díaz Ariño 2005: 234 nos 58-59; Fernández Gómez 2009: 150 no. 25.
[48] Caes. *Bell. Alex.* 61.
[49] Caes. *Bell. Hisp.* 3.
[50] Newspaper report in *El Español* (16 January 2020).

Excavations at Urso (Osuna), in 1903 and more recently, on a stretch of the town's walls yielded a wide range of military equipment suggesting an attack in 45 BC by a Caesarian force on this known Pompeian stronghold.[51] Finds included a number of lead bullets, most uninscribed but some with the letters CN MAG / IMP (Figure 20.3), which must have been shot, or been intended to be shot, by the Pompeian side.[52] The excavations also yielded *ballista* balls inscribed with Roman numerals.[53]

Early in 45 BC Caesar laid siege to the hilltop town of Ategua south of Córdoba which was supporting the Pompeian cause. Siegeworks mentioned in the ancient sources remain visible.[54] Sling bullets inscribed with the name of Gnaeus Pompeius (in the forms CN·MAG and CN·MAG·IMP) have been found.[55] Caesar mentions Latin texts inscribed on two lead bullets aimed at his forces. The first was an offer by one of the besieged soldiers to surrender when Caesar attacked.[56] The second detailed the defensive capabilities of the besieged.[57] The texts were presumably incised after firing, not inscribed in moulds. The necessarily brief wording was doubtless expanded by Caesar in his written account to render the message fully comprehensible. The town fell in February 45. Some bullets found in Southern Spain call on the god Jupiter for his support in battle.[58]

The battle of Munda, 45 BC

Caesar's final battle against the sons of the late Pompey was fought at Munda between Seville and Córdoba on 17 March 45 BC. Slingers are not specifically mentioned in the literary sources, but lead bullets attest their presence. The battle's location was long debated.[59] However, from the discovery of the bullets, it can be localised near Lantejuela (Figure 25), south-west of Astigi (Écija).

Though the battlefield doubtless extended over a wide area, one fixed point is the Cerro de la Balas ('Hill of the Bullets') midway between Astigi (Écija) and Urso (Osuna). The Cerro de las Balas has yielded many sling bullets held in museums. A group of up

---

[51] Engel and Paris 1906; Corzo Sánchez 1977; Ruiz Cecilia 2015: 475.
[52] Quesada Sanz 2008; Díaz Ariño 2008: 255 nos G31-38.
[53] Díaz Ariño 2008: 260 nos PC30-44.
[54] Caes. *Bell. Hisp.* 6-7; Dio 43.33.2. See Blanco Freijeiro 1983; Corzo Sánchez 1986.
[55] Díaz Ariño 2005: 234 nos 25-49 and 51-56. Bullets with this inscription are frequently advertised for sale on the internet.
[56] *Quo die ad oppidum capiundum accederent, se scutum esse positurum.* 'On the day [the Caesarians] would draw near, intending the capture of the town, he would lay down his shield' (Caes. *Bell. Hisp.* 13). By the mention of a *scutum*, a legionary's shield may be indicated.
[57] *Indicium glande scriptum misit, per quod certior fieret Caesar quae in oppido ad defendendum compararentur.* 'He sent information inscribed on a sling bullet, to make Caesar better aware of what was being prepared in the town for its defence' (Caes. *Bell. Hisp.* 18).
[58] *CIL* II²/5 1347 = Díaz Ariño 2008: 230 no. G18. For the equivalent Greek phrase, see Benedetti 2012b: 377 no. VI, 57c.
[59] Durán Recio 2002: 42; Ferreiro López 2005; Grünewald and Richter 2009: 451.

Civil war 1: Caesar against Pompey and his sons, 49-45 BC

Figure 26. Silver *denarius* depicting Julius Caesar, 44 BC. The coin legend reads: CAESAR·DICT·PERPETVO (Caesar, dictator for life). Photo: © The Hunterian, University of Glasgow (GLAHM 22531).

to 59 bullets, published in 2006,[60] contained multiple examples of four inscriptions: 17 naming Gnaeus Pompeius (Figures 1, 20.3), six a legion XIII (Figure 20.4),[61] and ten the single letter A.[62] Twenty-three were stamped with the letters *DD* (Figure 20.5).[63] A further three bullets were uninscribed. That *DD* stands for *decreto decurionum* ('by decree of the town councillors'), seems inevitable. The unnamed town is perhaps Munda. It looks as though the bullets in this group were all shot by the Pompeian side. We could suppose that the Cerro de las Balas was a Caesarian strongpoint being targeted, unless it was a Pompeian encampment where the bullets were being made.

Also to be associated with this battle are bullets reading AVF, with the letters ligatured.[64] The distribution is confined to a relatively small area. We could think of an individual's name. A number of bullets from the South of Spain bear the simple message *Acc(ipe)* 'take that', or, in one case, *Cae(sar), acc(ipe)*, 'Caesar, take that,' the

---

[60] Grünewald and Richter 2006; Pina Polo and Zanier 2006; cf. Grünewald and Richter 2009; Pina Polo and Zanier 2009. I follow Pina Polo and Zanier in assigning all the bullets to 45 BC. Grünewald and Richter place some at the time of the Second Punic War.
[61] A legion XIII was among Pompeian forces at this time (Caes. *Bell. Hisp.* 34).
[62] Perhaps for Ategua or Astigi.
[63] Pina Polo and Zanier 2006: 34; Díaz Ariño 2008: 253 no. G23.
[64] Díaz Ariño 2005: 234 nos 66-71; Díaz Ariño 2008: 254 no. G30; Fernández Gómez 2009: 148 no. 10.

latter clearly shot from the Pompeian side.[65] Two lead bullets found South-East of Córdoba, which are stamped with the letters M·C·P, may relate to the same battle; perhaps they report a person's abbreviated name, or that of a town.[66] A bullet from La Puebla de Cazalla (south-west of Lantejuela) reads: T·BEIV / PEOIO.[67] One side can be interpreted as the name T(itus) Beiu(s). The *nomen* Beius is rare.[68] The other side is more problematical. We might expect a military rank or a surname (*cognomen*), though soldiers rarely bore them in the Late Republic.[69]

The little-known town of Asso (Figure 19), at Murviedro de Lorca, south-west of Murcia, Spain, has yielded about 500 uninscribed lead bullets, of three distinct shapes, found just outside the town's stone wall, which are suggested as belonging to this time.[70] A total of 49 bullets, all uninscribed, were recovered by fieldwalking at the multi-period Alto dos Cacos ('The Hill of the Potsherds') in the Lower Tagus valley, Portugal, along with Roman military equipment. The site is suggested as a temporary camp datable to either 61-60 or 49-45 BC.[71]

---

[65] Díaz Ariño 2005: 234 nos 61-65; *ILLRP* 1105. Cf. Fortnum 1864: 270.
[66] Perea Yébenes 1997; Díaz Ariño 2008: 252 no. G19.
[67] Garcia Garrido and Lalana 1993: 104; Díaz Ariño 2005: 235 no. 88; Díaz Ariño 2008: 253 no. G20.
[68] *CIL* VI 10062 = *ILS* 5282.
[69] A bullet said to come from Urso (Osuna) reads MEP / NA (*CIL* II²/ 5 1106), which we could easily suppose preserves another Roman name (Díaz Ariño 2008: 253 no. G21). However, the same text occurs at other sites, particularly at Olynthus, Greece (Robinson 1942: 429 nos 2217-2218), where the bullets are datable to 348 BC, so that an association with events of the Late Republic in Spain is unlikely. For an example now at Trieste, see Mainardis 2007: 871 no.6.
[70] Fontenla Ballesta 2005. The circumstances of discovery are not specified.
[71] Pimenta *et al.* 2012: 99. Cf. Gomes *et al.* 2017.

Chapter 5

Civil war 2: Caesar's heirs and successors, 44-42 BC

The complicated political and military manoeuvrings in the months after Caesar's assassination in March 44 BC are well documented in the rich literary record of the period.[1] Caesar's assassins, optimistically entitling themselves the Liberators, took command of provinces and armies east of the Adriatic, while his supporters, Mark Antony and his great-nephew and heir, the young Octavian, who was to be the future emperor Augustus, held Italy and the west. The army in Macedonia, which Caesar had intended to lead against the Parthians, comprised six legions.[2] Antony obtained control over them and began transferring them westwards across the Adriatic.

The battle of Mutina, 43 BC

Before the end of 44 Decimus Junius Brutus, the governor of Cisalpine Gaul (Northern Italy), was challenged for his position by Mark Antony. Brutus retired within the walls of Mutina (Modena), a town in his province on the *Via Aemilia* between Bononia (Bologna) and Parma (Figure 27). Antony, on arrival soon after, 'ditched and walled off the town', presumably with a circumvallation.[3]

From a combination of literary records and inscriptions we can reconstruct the forces present. Decimus Brutus had four legions and a force of gladiators. Octavian and the consul Aulus Hirtius, who arrived at Mutina in March 43, had the *legio Martia* and a legion IIII, both of which had defected from Antony, and three other legions, of which two (VII and VIII) were of recalled veterans, which Octavian himself had re-formed in Campania. We chance to have the gravestone at Teanum (Teano) in Campania of a veteran of legion VIII, which is entitled *Mutinensis*, written out in full, surely referring to events in 43 BC.[4] Antony retained two of the legions recently transferred from Macedonia, II and XXXV, as well as the veteran V *Alaudae*. The other consul, C. Vibius Pansa, soon arrived from Rome, bringing with him four newly-raised legions, likely to have been numbered I-IIII. An inscription at the colony of Astigi (Écija) in Southern Spain names a legion II *Pansiana*, which was presumably among them.[5]

Leaving his younger brother Lucius Antonius (on whom see below p. 53) to maintain the siege of Mutina, in April 43 BC Mark Antony's forces clashed with the legions of the consuls Hirtius and Pansa, who were acting in concert with the young Octavian,

---

[1] Botermann 1969; Osgood 2006: 47.
[2] Brunt 1971: 480.
[3] App. *BC* 3.49; cf. Dio 46.36.
[4] *CIL* X 4786 = *ILS* 2239. See Keppie 1983: 140.
[5] *AE* 2001, 1204. See now Keppie 2022.

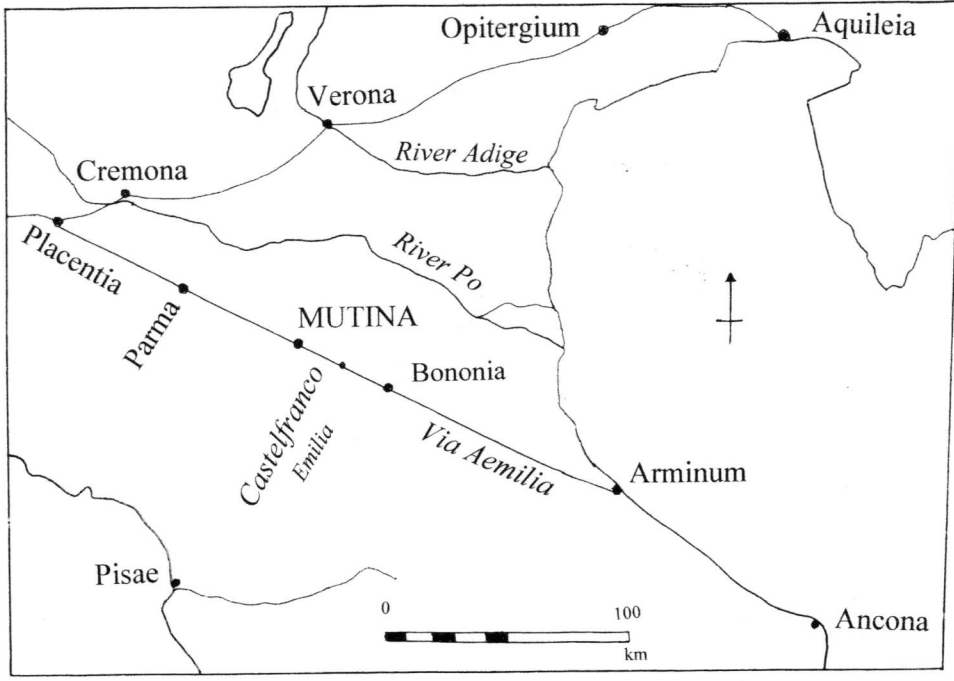

Figure 27. Northern Italy, showing location of Mutina (Modena).

on the Senate's behalf.[6] Antony had at his disposal a considerable body of cavalry,[7] but slingers are not mentioned. The fighting raged fiercely at Forum Gallorum (Castelfranco Emilia), a village south of Mutina, where the marshy site became littered with corpses and discarded military equipment.[8] Antony fell back to Mutina where the two sides met again, a week later, outside the walls of the town. Antony was forced to retire north-westwards into Gaul.

A total of about 30 lead bullets have been found at or near Mutina, a few of them inscribed.[9] There are two main groups. The first can be associated with the fighting at Forum Gallorum and helps to localise the battle, at which Pansa was mortally wounded. One bullet, now lost, appeared to read L II / L IV, which can be expanded to *l(egio)* II / *l(egio)* IV, the names being evidently inscribed on different sides of the bullet. If correctly read, this would be the only known single bullet to name two legions. Both seem likely to have been among the consular forces.[10] A second lost bullet read

---

[6] Fields 2018.
[7] Cic. *Fam.* 10.30.2.
[8] App. *BC* 3.70. See Solari 1939; Manfredi 1975.
[9] See D'Ercole and Savi 2017, where their findspots are identified.
[10] Antony too had a legion II but not a legion IIII.

Civil war 2: Caesar's heirs and successors, 44-42 BC

Figure 28. Gold *aureus* depicting Octavian, 42 BC. The coin legend reads: C·CAESAR·III·VIR·R· P·C (Gaius Caesar, Triumvir for the ordering of the state). Photo: © The Hunterian, University of Glasgow (GLAHM 22579).

M·ANTO, clearly naming Mark Antony; it was presumably shot by his side.[11] A third read P·IR, not yet explained.[12] A single bullet from a farmstead near Castelfranco reads NAT ACC COSS, probably to be understood as *natibus accipite, consules* ('Take [this] on the buttocks, consuls').[13] This bullet must have been shot from the Antonian side, aimed at the consuls Hirtius and Pansa. The mention of buttocks presupposes flight from the battlefield.[14]

The second group comprises a number of uninscribed bullets found at or near Mutina itself, and could relate to the second battle, in which Hirtius was killed, or be linked to siege operations.[15] Some weaponry is also reported. Other bullets found several kilometres outside Mutina may serve to localise scenes of fighting or the sites of camps, to which the literary sources testify.[16]

---

[11] D'Ercole and Savi 2017: 367.
[12] D'Ercole and Savi 2017: *loc.cit.*, where it is suggested that this text preserves the name of a P(ublius) [H]irtius, an otherwise unknown relative of the consul Aulus Hirtius.
[13] D'Ercole and Savi 2017: 368. I am grateful for this expansion of the text to Professors J.N. Adams and R.P.H. Green.
[14] Pritchett 1991: 62.
[15] Three found north-west of the town at Parco Novi Sad and one to the south in Viale Amendola (D'Ercole and Savi 2017: 368). A group of 14 uninscribed bullets were found in Viale Reiter inside the town in the course of an excavation, together with other material including lamps and amphorae (Labate *et al.* 2012; D'Ercole and Savi 2017: 368 figura 2).
[16] App. *BC* 3.71. Two other bullets, one inscribed FERI ('strike'), are reported. See www.mutinaromana.it/

Figure 29. Silver *denarius* naming Q. Salvidienus Rufus and showing a lightning-bolt, 40 BC. The coin legend reads: Q·SALVIVS·IMP·COS·DESIG (Quintus Salvius, saluted as victorious commander, consul designate). Photo: © The Hunterian, University of Glasgow (GLAHM 22687).

Events of 42 BC: Calabria, Sicily, Philippi

Subsequently Octavian became reconciled to Antony and, in conjunction with the proconsul M. Aemilius Lepidus, formed in November 43 a momentous alliance, the 'Triumvirate for the ordering of the state' (See Figures 28, 37).

Sling bullets have illuminated the activity of Octavian's legate Q. Salvidienus Rufus (named on coins as Q. Salvius Rufus) in Calabria in early 42.[17] From Cassius Dio we know that Salvidienus drove Sextus Pompeius, Pompey's surviving son, out of mainland Italy, for which he was saluted as *imperator* (victorious Roman commander), but was subsequently worsted in a sea battle off Tauromenium (Taormina), on Sicily's east coast, which allowed Sextus to take full control of the island (Figure 30).[18]

Salvidienus Rufus is named on sling bullets found on both sides of the Strait of Messina: at Leucopetra, a promontory on the mainland 20 kms south of Rhegium (Reggio), at Vibo Valentia in Calabria and at Catana (Catania) and Syracusae (Syracuse) on Sicily's

---

lesercito/lartiglieria (Accessed 16 December 2022), where they are illustrated.
[17] Costabile 1985.
[18] App. *BC* 4.85; Dio 48.18.

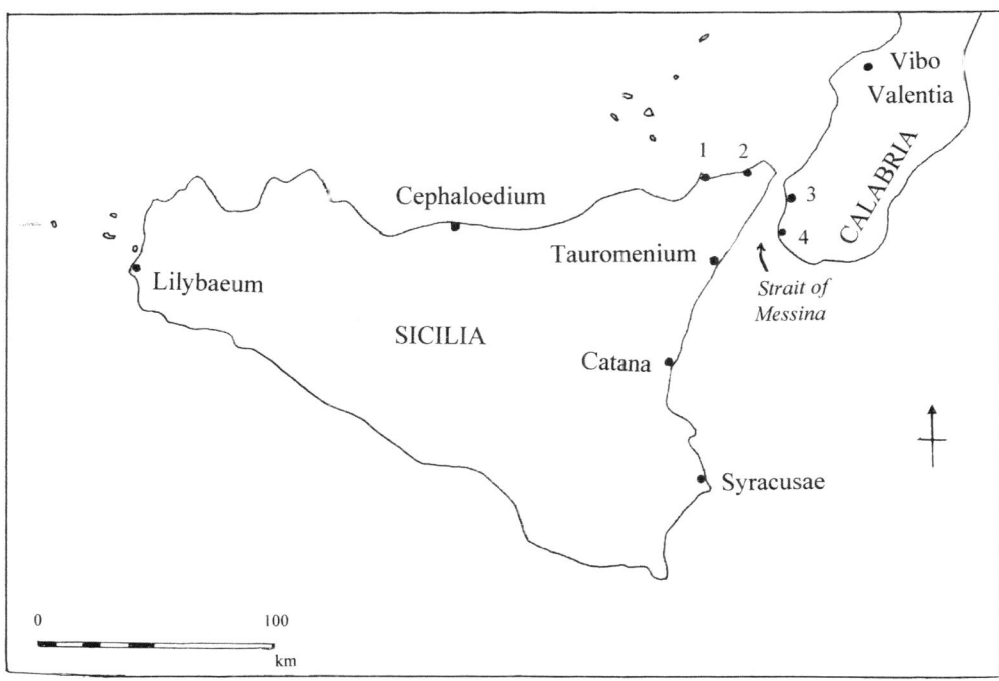

Figure 30. Sicily and Calabria (Italy), to illustrate events in 42-36 BC. Note: 1. Mylae; 2. Naulochus; 3. Rhegium; 4. Leucopetra.

east coast.[19] Conceivably they testify to the location of fighting in 42, or to points of embarkation. Slingers must have been among the troops available to Salvidienus. The bullets bearing his name use the form Q·SAL·IM, Q(uintus) Sal(vius) im(perator) (Figure 18.7).[20] His coins and some of the bullets carry a lightning-bolt emblem, which is sometimes considered his personal symbol (Figure 29),[21] but the lightning-bolt appears regularly on bullets at this time, including those shot by Octavian's troops at Perusia.[22]

A total of ten bullets naming Salvidienus are known (Figure 18.7). One of those found at Leucopetra names a legion X.[23] Under the Empire, one of the two legions with this numeral bore the title *Fretensis*, which is normally taken as alluding to events of 36 BC in and around the *Fretum Siculum* (Strait of Messina). The legion had among its emblems

---

[19] *CIL* X 8337A = *ILLRP* 1120. See Costabile 1985; Buoncore 1989: 44.
[20] For the man and his career see Rohr Vio 1999. He is named as 'Rufus' on sling bullets at Perusia, see (Figure 32.3).
[21] Münzer 1920: 2019; Schmitthenner 1958: 68.
[22] Benedetti 2012a: nos 3-8.
[23] Zangemeister 1885: no. 2a = Costabile 1985: 369 no. 8.

a dolphin and a galley,[24] clear indicators of involvement in a naval battle. However, the bullet at Leucopetra could indicate the legion's participation in earlier fighting in 42 BC under Salvidienus Rufus; the award of the title *Fretensis* may therefore belong then. A sling bullet naming a legion X, 'procured' in Sicily by a nineteenth-century Anglican clergyman, the Reverend William Falconer, appeared to report C·VARRO / 7·L X, i.e. 'Gaius Varro, centurion in legion X'; passed to the collector C.D.E.Fortnum (on whom see below p. 57), the bullet is now in The Ashmolean, Oxford.[25] In this context mention can be made of a bullet found at Saint-Pargoire in the South of France, which reads C·VARI 7· L X, i.e. 'Gaius Varius, centurion in legion X' (Figure 18.6).[26] This could even be the same man.[27] The findspot lies on the border between the territories of Baeterrae (Béziers) and Nemausus (Nîmes).[28] The bullet must date to the Late Republic, but it cannot be assigned to any particular campaign or battle. Veterans of Caesar's legion X were settled in 46-45 BC at Narbo Martius (Narbonne) further to the south-west.

Later in 42, Antony's and Octavian's legions clashed with those of the Liberators, Brutus and Cassius, outside the town of Philippi (Filippoi) in north-eastern Greece.[29] Slingers, archers and stone-throwers were, it seems, active on both sides.[30] After a hard-fought battle in two phases, extending over several weeks, the Liberators were defeated. The site of the battle has been disputed, and no sling bullets appear to have been recovered.[31]

---

[24] Keppie 1984: 208.
[25] Fortnum 1864: 270. This bullet (The Ashmolean, no. V.243) has recently been assigned to Perugia; see www.latininscriptions.ashmus.ox.ac.uk (accessed 16 December 2022).
[26] Feugère 2008 has a map to illustrate the findspot.
[27] I could discern only the letters VAR; the inscription is partially obscured by the museum's display-mounting.
[28] Mauné 2012: 496.
[29] Sheppard 2008.
[30] App. *BC* 4.12; Dio 47.43.
[31] Butera and Sears 2017.

Chapter 6

The siege of Perusia, 41-40 BC

In the late summer of 41 Octavian and his lieutenants shut up Lucius Antonius, Mark Antony's younger brother, who was one of the consuls of the year, in the Umbrian hilltop town of Perusia (Perugia), and enclosed it with extensive siegeworks, including a circumvallation and numerous wooden towers (Figure 31).[1] No trace of these works has ever been located on the ground or from the air. Slingers are reported in Lucius' army during an abortive attempt to break through Octavian's (i.e. Caesarian) siegelines.[2]

Inscribed lead sling bullets have been reported at Perusia over a long period.[3] Those found up to 1885 were authoritatively published by Karl Zangemeister.[4] The museum at Perugia holds a number of bullets not present in Zangemeister's corpus, but when and in what circumstances they were found seems unknown. Some of those no longer traceable are known from photographs of the later nineteenth century.[5] Three more were, surprisingly, found in 1956 during the excavation of a Late Roman bath-house at Montferrand in South-West France;[6] these are suggested as souvenirs carried to a distant location by soldiers present at the siege.[7] Another was picked up in a field at Glons in Belgium.[8]

A total of more than 180 sling bullets are now known, which from the texts they bear were shot by both sides (Figures 32-33, 35). Hardly any enjoy a secure provenance, except that one was first reported near Monteluce north-east of Perugia.[9] A group of 37 bullets from the grounds of a monastery outside the city's wall is discussed separately (below, p. 58). A large number are held in the Museo Archeologico Nazionale dell'Umbria at Perugia.[10] Others are in the Museo Nazionale Romano in Rome,[11] and a few in other museums in Italy and France. A dozen are in The Ashmolean, Oxford (see below p. 57). In 2012 Lucio Benedetti published a welcome catalogue of the surviving examples.[12]

---

[1] App. *BC* 5.32. For accounts of the Perusine War, see Gabba 1971; Wallmann 1975.
[2] App. *BC* 5.36.
[3] Henry 1972: volume 1, 118, 152; Mangiameli 2012: 197.
[4] Zangemeister 1885: nos 52-108.
[5] E.g. Zangemeister 1885: no. 79 tabula ix.5 = Figure 32.8.
[6] Passelac 2006; *AE* 2009, 851-853.
[7] Benedetti 2012b: 385 no. VI, 57s.
[8] Brulet and Lepot 2018.
[9] Benedetti 2012a: no. 40.
[10] Benedetti 2012a: 47-48.
[11] Benedetti 2012a: 48; 2012b: 375.
[12] Benedetti 2012a.

Figure 31. Perusia (Perugia, Italy). Panoramic view from the North-West, showing the Basilica of San Domenico (centre), with the bell-tower of the Abbazia of San Pietro further towards the right. Photo: trolvag. Wikimedia Commons. Licence: CC BY-SA 3.0 Unported.

Some bullets name commanders present at the siege, such as Octavian (Figure 32.5) and his legate Q. Salvidienus Rufus (Figure 32.3), but not Octavian's right-hand man M. Vipsanius Agrippa, known to have been present, or indeed Lucius Antonius.[13] On Caesarian bullets Octavian is called *imperator Caesar*;[14] by contrast those shot by the forces of Lucius Antonius call him *Octavius*, thereby denying his adoption by Julius Caesar.[15] Mark Antony is named on two bullets manifestly shot outwards by the defenders (Figure 32.4);[16] but neither he nor his wife Fulvia (see below) were present in the town.

The literary sources do not give a detailed breakdown of the forces present; the inscribed lead bullets are our principal guide. They have long testified to legions numbered IIII, VI, VII, XI and XII;[17] one bullet of legion XII has the title *Victrix*, otherwise unattested (Figure 32.6).[18] Benedetti's recent catalogue confirms that we should add VIII.[19] Another, inscribed with the name of legion XI, reads *Divom Iulium*, praising

---

[13] Except for bullets directed at him (Zangemeister 1885: nos 64-65 = *ILLRP* 1111-1112); Benedetti 2012a: no. 33.
[14] Benedetti 2012a: nos 26-28.
[15] Benedetti 2012a: nos 29-31.
[16] Benedetti 2012a: nos 1-2.
[17] Benedetti 2012a: 44; *ILLRP* 1114-1117a.
[18] Benedetti 2012a: no. 40. For another record of a legion XII, see De Minicis 1844: Tabula II, 63; Zangemeister 1885: 82 no. 112.
[19] Benedetti 2012a: no. 39.

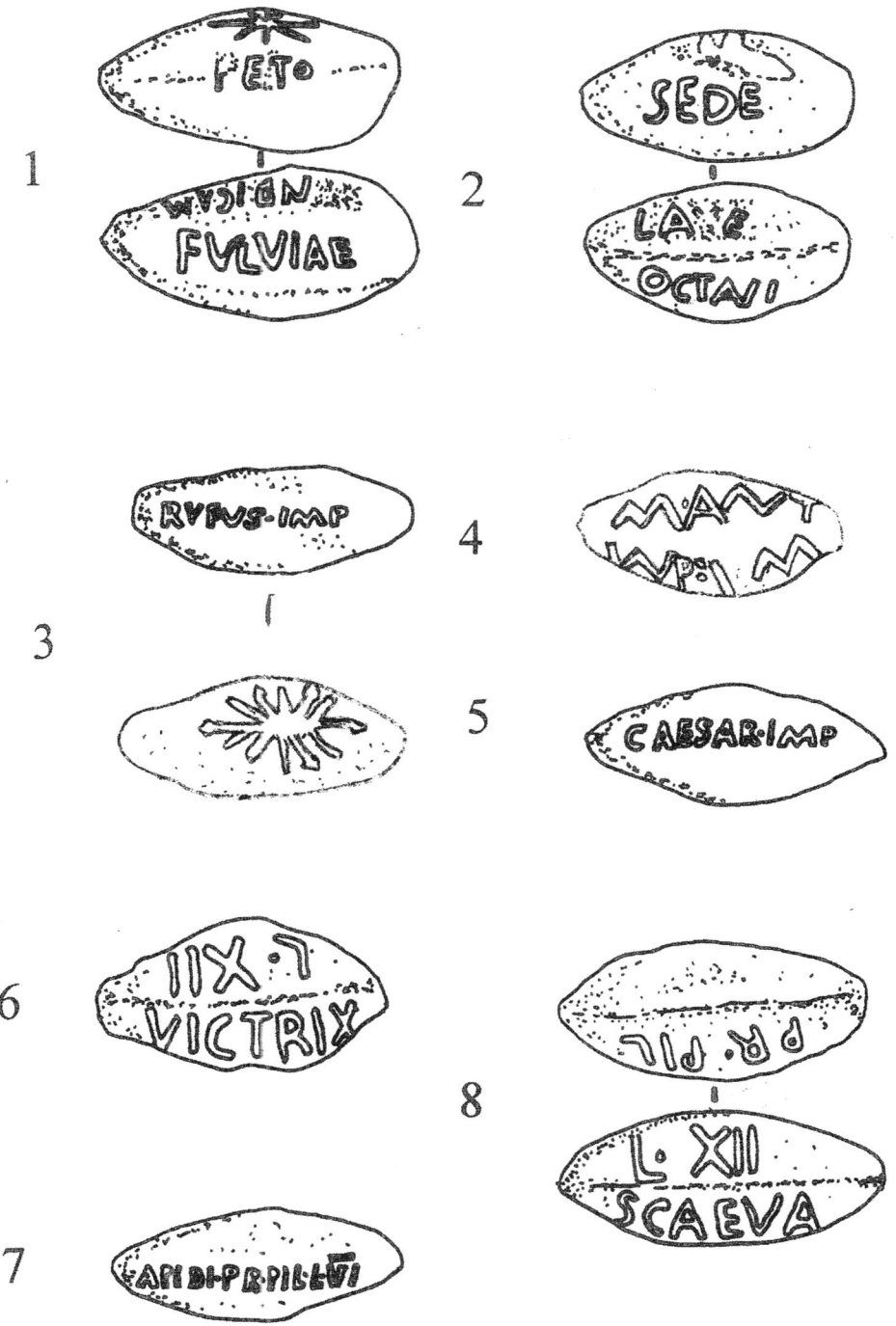

Figure 32. Lead sling bullets from Perusia (Italy), 41-40 BC. After Keppie (nos 1-3 front, 5-8; Benedetti (nos 3 back, 4). Scale 1:1.

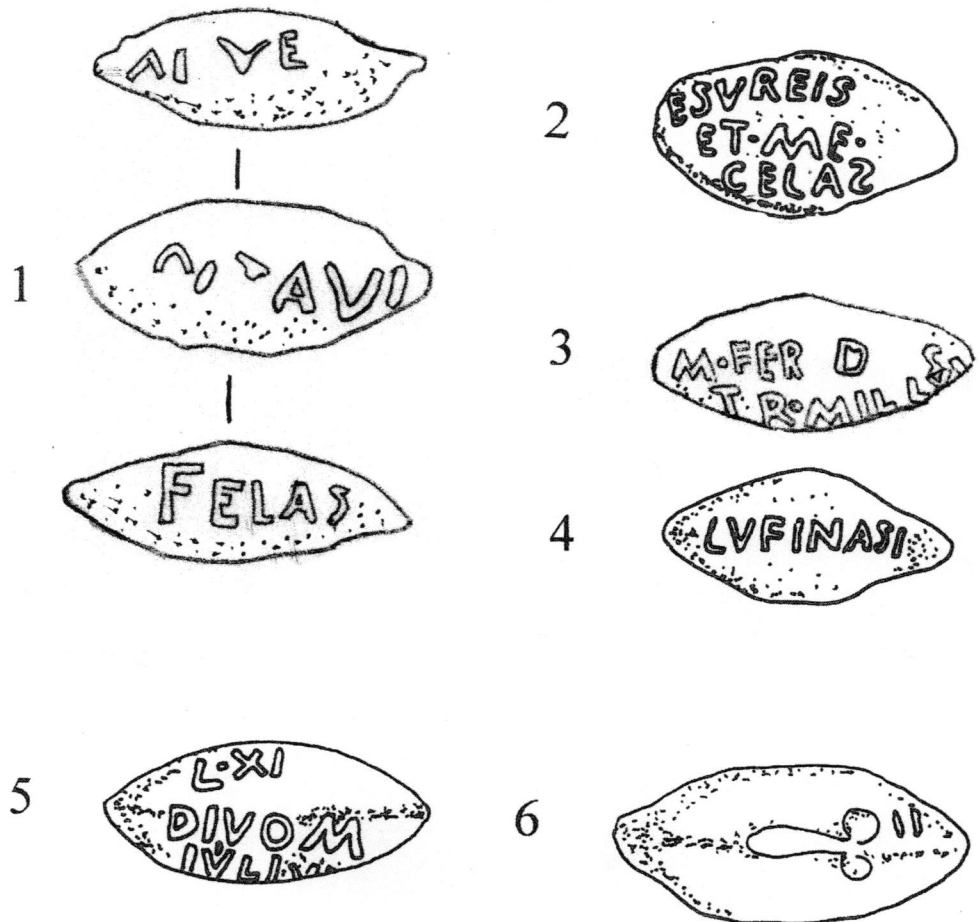

Figure 33. Lead sling bullets from Perusia (Italy), 41-40 BC. After Benedetti (nos 1, 3); Keppie nos 2, 4-6). Scale 1:1.

the now deified Caesar, clearly in the accusative case with a verb such as *ulciscor* ('I avenge') to be understood (Figure 33.5).[20] Several of the legions are identifiable as Caesar's re-formed veteran legions.[21] L. Antonius' legions are likely to be numbered no higher than VI, six being the total number raised by him at the beginning of his consulship.[22] Veterans were re-enlisted on both sides.

---

[20] Zangemeister 1885: no. 77 = *ILLRP* 1116. Cf. Zangemeister 1885: no. 78. For *Divos Iulius* on coins, see Rowan 2019: 63 figure 3.10.
[21] Schmitthenner 1958: 65; Keppie 1984: 132. A legion XII *Gallica* has recently been reported (*AE* 2017, 437).
[22] App. *BC* 5.24. See now Keppie 2022: 194.

Inscriptions on surviving bullets name M. Feridius, tribune of legion XI (Figure 33.3), Apidius, *primus pilus* of legion VI (Figure 32.7), and T. Etrius, *primus pilus* of legion IIII.[23] Apidius' name is abbreviated in various ways, sometimes even to AP without naming his legion.[24] Scaeva, surely Caesar's famous centurion, is recorded as *primus pilus* of legion XII (Figure 32.8).[25] The names of other likely officers are unfortunately illegible.[26] There are no certain examples of lower-ranking centurions or of ordinary legionaries being named.[27]

Three bullets, one first reported in Rome and the other two now at Verona, bear the inscription T·FABRICIVS / FECIT ('Titus Fabricius made [this]).'[28] An association with Perugia has been suggested.[29] Benedetti argued that Fabricius, who is not accorded any military rank, was a manufacturer supplying various combatants.[30]

The online publication of the small collection of inscribed lead bullets held by The Ashmolean, Oxford, is particularly opportune.[31] The group was bequeathed to it in 1899 by C.D.E. Fortnum,[32] who had acquired the bullets at Perugia or at Rome. Legions VI and XII, which they record,[33] were already known, but the Ashmolean bullets may also name V and XV.[34] On the other hand, the proposed record of legion X *Equestris*,[35] is in my view, unjustified. The first line of text appears to read ALXE but the meaning is unclear (see also p. 59 footnote 51). Legion X *Equestris* is identifiable as Caesar's Tenth, his favourite in Gaul. It was re-formed after his death and served with Mark Antony in the East in the decade between Philippi and Actium.[36]

---

[23] Benedetti 2012a: nos 14-22. In 52 BC Marcus Caelius recommended a Marcus Feridius to Cicero, as a *bonum et strenuum adulescentem*, 'a good and vigorous young man' (Cic. *Fam.* 8.9.4).
[24] Benedetti 2012a: nos 17-22; Brulet and Lepot 2018.
[25] Zangemeister 1885: no. 79 tabula ix.5 = *ILLRP* 1116a. In 48 BC Scaeva had been made *primus pilus* of legion VI. For Scaeva see also above p. 41.
[26] Benedetti 2012a: nos 63-71. The Latin personal names on bullets at Perugia are generally given in the nominative case (e.g. *ILLRP* 1113), thus emphasising the authority of the issuers; however, the centurions' names appear to be in the genitive case (Benedetti 2012a: nos 15-22), unless their *nomina* have been abbreviated to save space. The genitive case is used by the Aetolian slingers at Numantia (above p. 12; Figure 13.3), and on some of the 'legionary' coins issued by Mark Antony in 32-31 BC.
[27] For stone *ballista* balls of Augustan date at Qasr Ibrim, Egypt, painted with the names of centurions in the genitive case, see Wilkins 2017: 118 fig. 106.
[28] Benedetti 2012b: 378 no.VI, 57e; Buonopane 2014; *AE* 2015, 472a and b. For a modern forgery, see Benedetti 2012b: 689 no. X, 5.
[29] Völling 1990: 41.
[30] Benedetti 2012b: 378 no. VI, 57e. A similar text, on a bullet found at Montferrand in the South of France, names Q. Vo[...] (*AE* 2009, 853).
[31] See 'The Ashmolean Latin Inscriptions Project', under the direction of Prof. A. E. Cooley (www.latininscriptions.ashmus.ox.ac.uk). Accessed 16 December 2022.
[32] Fortnum 1864; 1870. Benedetti knew of these bullets (2012a: 51), but not of their survival at The Ashmolean.
[33] The Ashmolean, nos V.242, 253, 259.
[34] The Ashmolean, nos V.248, 250, 254, 255.
[35] www.latininscriptions.ashmus.ox.ac.uk, at V.241.
[36] On legion X *Equestris*, see Keppie 2000: 84.

Several bullets at Perugia bear the letters LVFINASIA, with slight variant readings (Figure 33.4).[37] Zangemeister knew of 15 examples, all from the grounds of the Abbazia of San Pietro outside the town to the south-east (Figure 31).[38] They were found together at a depth of 80 cms from the modern surface. Another 22 bullets from this location were uninscribed; none of the latter appear to survive. Some of the bullets exhibited apparent signs of use, others not. A number of different moulds were distinguished.[39] Their discovery in a single location some distance outside the walls of the town suggests a quantity prepared but never used. The findspot may indicate that they belonged to the besiegers.

No satisfactory explanation of LVFINASIA has ever been advanced.[40] Benedetti suggested the name *L. Ufin(ius) Asia(ticus* or *-nus)*, but this fails to convince.[41] An equally improbable alternative could be *Lu(ci) f(uga) in Asia(m)* ('Lucius, flee to Asia'), the reference being to the Roman province of Asia, at that time controlled by Mark Antony.[42] However, as there are no interpuncts on most of the bullets, this may be a single (otherwise unknown) word.[43]

Several bullets at Perugia carry a lightning-bolt symbol, sometimes accompanied by an inscription. The lightning-bolt is found on bullets naming Octavian, Salvidienus Rufus, two of the legions, VI and XI, and on one bullet directed against Fulvia.[44] It has sometimes been supposed that that the lightning-bolt was the special emblem of Salvidienus Rufus (above p. 51), serving here to identify legions under his command even when the man himself was not named, but the evidence does not support this.[45]

A small number of bullets at Perugia carry sexual insults, more perhaps if their texts could be better understood.[46] A *phallus* appears alone on two bullets (Figure 33.6).[47] Caesarian bullets are rude about Lucius Antonius, and Antonian bullets about Octavian. The latter's sexual orientation is disputed and his alleged lewd practices highlighted.[48] A few bullets were aimed at tender parts of the male and female anatomy. A bullet reading PETO / [LA]NDICAM / FVLVIAE, 'I'm aimed at Fulvia's fanny', was manifestly shot from the Caesarian side (Figure 32.1),[49] and PET(O)

---

[37] Benedetti 2012a: nos 44-55.
[38] Zangemeister 1885: nos 86-88.
[39] Zangemeister 1885: at no. 86.
[40] Two bullets have L·VFINASIA, as though the inscriber evidently believed that the initial letter L was, as so often elsewhere, abbreviated from the word *legio*.
[41] Benedetti 2012a: 81 at no. 44.
[42] Benedetti 2012a: *loc.cit.*
[43] For the word *fuga* incised on a stone *ballista* ball at Calagurris (Calahorra), Spain, see above p. 26.
[44] Benedetti 2012a: nos 3-14, 17-19, 26-28, 32, 64, 71, 74-77.
[45] For a clay mould from Paris with the inscription *fulg(ur)* ('lightning'), see above p. 7.
[46] Benedetti 2012a: nos 29-32 = *ILLRP* 1108-1109. See Hallett 1977.
[47] Benedetti 2012a: nos 72, 78; cf. no. 29.
[48] Hallett 1977: 157. For the poems composed at this time by Octavian against Fulvia, see Martial *Ep.* 11.20. Lefebvre 2018 considers the sexual content of the bullets.
[49] Benedetti 2012a: no. 32, cf. no. 60. For the use of the word *landica* see Adams 1982: 97.

Figure 34. Silver *denarius* depicting Lucius Antonius, 41 BC. The coin legend reads: L·ANTONIVS·COS (Lucius Antonius, consul). Photo: Classical Numismatic Group. Inc. Wikimedia Commons. Licence: CC BY-SA 3.0 Unported.

/ OCTAV[I]A / CVLVM, translated as 'I'm aiming for Octavian's arse,'[50] from the Antonian side. Another includes the words OCTAVI / FELAS, 'Octavius, you cocksucker' (Figure 33.1).[51] Yet another reads: LAXE / OCTAVI / SEDE, apparently 'Limp Octavius, settle yourself down (on me)', accompanied by the illustration of a *phallus* (Figure 32.2).[52] Another, now lost, insults both Lucius and Fulvia in a single text: L·A·CALVE / FVLVIA / CVLVM PAN[DITE], 'Bald L(ucius) A(ntonius) (and) Fulvia, open wide your

---

[50] Benedetti 2012a: no. 31. The reading is clear, its meaning less so. The Antonians besieged inside Perusia were unlikely to use the name Octavian (implying acceptance of his adoption by Julius Caesar), and it has been suggested that calling him Octavia was to draw attention to his effeminacy (Hallett 1977: 152). Alternatively, could the reference be to Octavian's elder sister who was in due course to become Mark Antony's next wife?

[51] Zangemeister 1885: no. 60. The complete text reads: ALXE / OCTAVI / FELAS. Two examples are known, from different moulds, one in The Ashmolean (no. V.241), the other in the Museo Archeologico, Perugia (Benedetti 2012a: no 30 tavola 17). The letters ALXE seem clear on the Ashmolean example (see also Fortnum 1864: 270), and can be read on the bullet at Perugia; the word [S]ALVE, 'Greetings', has been restored (Zangemeister 1885: no. 60), recalling the sarcastic wording on a bullet at Asculum (Zangemeister 1885: no. 10). For usage of the verb *fellare*, see Adams 1983: 130.

[52] Benedetti 2012a: no. 29; cf. no. 58.

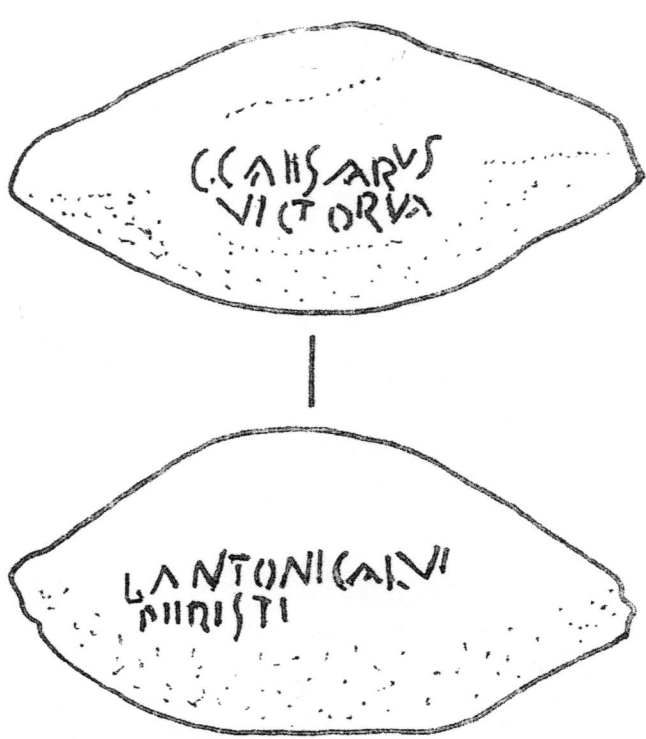

Figure 35. Lead sling bullet from Perusia (Italy), 41-40 BC.
After Benedetti. Scale 2:1.

arses.'[53] Lucius' baldness is a feature unreported in the literary sources but confirmed by coinage (Figure 34).[54] The word *calvus* (bald) is used here almost like a *cognomen*. The Roman believed baldness indicated sexual inadequacy.[55] In fact Fulvia was then at Praeneste (Palestrina), south of Rome,[56] but Octavian's soldiers may have believed she was inside Perusia.[57] Some of the sexual messages were inscribed in moulds, so that wide circulation was intended. Another bullet addresses a recipient as PATHICE ('You sodomite').[58]

Particular attention attaches to a bullet bearing an inscription which combines confidence in Octavian's eventual victory with a jibe directed against Lucius Antonius.

---

[53] De Minicis 1844: tabula 2.45; CIL 1, 684; Zangemeister 1885: no. 65 = ILLRP 1112.
[54] Crawford 1974: no. 517.
[55] By contrast, Suet. *Caes.* 51 on Caesar's baldness.
[56] Dio 48.10.
[57] For verbal insults hurled at Sulla and his wife from the walls of Athens during the siege of 87-86 BC, see Plut. *Sull.* 13.1, *Mor.* 505b.
[58] Benedetti 2012a: no. 34.

It brings before us a keen supporter of Octavian, presumably a legionary (Figure 35). The minuscule letters were incised with a sharp implement on a blank bullet after casting. The inscription reads C·CAESARVS / VICTORIA / L·ANTONI CALVE / PERISTI, Gaius Caesar is the winner. Bald Lucius Antonius, you have lost.[59] The inscription provides us with a closely datable example of Latin handwriting, with letter-forms distinctive of the time.

Two bullets from Perusia read ESVREIS / ET·ME / CELAS, to be explained as 'You are hungry and are concealing it from me' (Figure 33.2).[60] The famine endured by the besieged became notorious. The town, with a large army to be fitted in, must have been very crowded; moreover the defenders had had no time to collect food in advance.[61] The same text recurs on two bullets (from a different mould) found at Montferrand, between Carcassonne and Toulouse in the South of France,[62] one of which has the additional text CASEVM / COMES / PERM, apparently 'I allow you cheese, comrade.'[63] The siege ended early in 40 BC, the defenders having been starved into submission. Lucius Antonius' legions were sent into winter quarters at unspecified locations.[64] They seem to have been incorporated forthwith into Octavian's forces, recent enmities presumably quickly forgotten.[65]

---

[59] Benedetti 2012a: no. 33 = ILLRP 1111. See Hallett 1977: 153 no. 5.
[60] See Benedetti 2012a: nos 35-36.
[61] App. BC 5. 34.
[62] Passelac 2006; AE 2009, 851-52.
[63] AE 2009, 851.
[64] App. BC 5.47.
[65] Brunt 1971: 496.

Chapter 7

From Perusia to Actium, 40-31 BC

The first half of the following decade, which culminated in the conclusive sea battle at Actium, was marked by the continuing threat from Sextus Pompeius in Sicily and more widely in the Western Mediterranean (Figure 36).[1] Lead bullets found on the west coast of Sicily, at Lilybaeum (Marsala),[2] and on its north coast at Cephaloedium (Cefalù),[3] are inscribed MAG·IMP, *Mag(nus) Imp(erator)*. They call to mind the numerous bullets from Southern Spain inscribed CN·MAG·IMP, which report Gnaeus Pompeius the Younger (above, p. 44). Here, however, the inscriptions must refer to Gnaeus' younger brother Sextus Pompeius, and testify to the presence of his troops.[4] In 36 BC

Figure 36. Gold *aureus* depicting Sextus Pompeius, 42-40 BC. The coin legend reads: MAG·PIVS·IMP·ITER (Magnus Pius, twice saluted victorious commander).
Photo: © The Hunterian, University of Glasgow (GLAHM 22653).

---

[1] A former tribune in a legion XII, T. Marius, served as a *praefectus* (squadron commander) in a fleet at about this time *in Sicilia* (*CIL* 11, 6058; Linderski 2002: 578; Osgood 2006: 272). Marius subsequently assumed the *cognomen* Siculus.
[2] Out of 61 bullets recovered from a cemetery area 200 m outside the walls of Lilybaeum, one read MAG IMP, another bore a lightning-bolt emblem (Bechtold *et al.* 1999: 184, tavola 40 nos 380-81).
[3] Zangemeister 1885: no. 2 = *CIL* X 8063.3.
[4] For his nomenclature on coins, see Crawford 1974: 520 no. 511; Rowan 2019: 72.

Figure 37. Silver *denarius* issued by Mark Antony, 32-31 BC. The obverse (above) shows a galley, the reverse (below) an eagle between two standards, celebrating his legion V. The coin legend reads (obverse): ANT·AVG·IIIVIR·R·P·C (Antonius, augur, Triumvir for the ordering of the state); (reverse): LEG V (legion V) Photo: © The Hunterian, University of Glasgow (GLAHM 22733).

Sextus was defeated in sea-battles at Mylae and Naulochus off the North-East coast of Sicily; fleeing to Asia Minor, he was executed in the following year.[5]

In 38 BC Octavian's trusted lieutenant, M. Vipsanius Agrippa, undertook a campaign in Aquitania, not yet a Roman province, in South-West France. Lead sling bullets, some of them bearing Agrippa's name in the forms M·AGR/IMP or M·AGRIP/IMP (*Marcus Agrippa imperator*) have been found in a hillfort attacked at L'Ermitage d'Agen, on his likely route down the valley of the River Garonne towards Bordeaux (Figure 18.8).[6] Once again the finds illustrate the potential of this form of evidence to elucidate scenes of fighting and the progress of armies on campaign.[7]

An inscribed lead bullet, found with others at Apsorus (Osor) on the small Dalmatian island of Crexi (Cres), may relate to an otherwise unknown siege of the town.[8] The inscription, in lettering datable to the Late Republic, scratched with a sharp-pointed implement (Figure 13.4), reads PERTINACIA / VOS·RADICITV[S] / TO[L]LET. 'Persistence will do away with (all of) you utterly'.[9] As the bullet was recovered inside the town, it may have been shot inwards by one of the attackers, but we know nothing of the circumstances.[10]

A hilltop site at Andagoste (Cuartango, in Alava province, North-East Spain), which seems likely to date within this decade, appears to be a Roman temporary camp, at the centre of a spread of military equipment, which looks to have come under attack; a total of over 110 uninscribed bullets were recovered.[11]

Octavian himself campaigned on the east side of the Adriatic between 35 and 33 BC. We are told that he was wounded in the knee by a stone.[12] A number of sites in modern Slovenia have yielded lead bullets, mostly uninscribed, which are likely to belong at this time and testify to Roman assaults on native strongholds.[13]

Mark Antony had remained in the East after the battle of Philippi, intending to take revenge on the Parthians for the ignominious defeat inflicted on the legions of M. Licinius Crassus at Carrhae in Syria in 53 BC, an expedition which Caesar himself had intended to lead. Antony's legate, P. Ventidius, conducted a successful campaign in

---

[5] App. *BC* 5.144.
[6] Verdin 2013: 94 figure 19.
[7] For the many uninscribed sling bullets found at Vieille-Toulouse which lay on his likely route, see Verdin 2013: 101.
[8] Zangemeister 1885: 81 no. 109; *CIL* I² 887 = *ILLRP* 1103. See Vitelli Casella 2019.
[9] I owe the translation to Prof. R.P.H. Green.
[10] For a discussion of possible contexts see Vitelli Casella 2019: 705. Another bullet, inscribed XXV or XXVI (Zangemeister 1885: 81 no. 110 = *CIL* I² 888), could, it is suggested, identify a participating legion. The other 20 bullets found at Apsorus were uninscribed.
[11] Unzueta Portilla 2006; Amela Valverde 2015.
[12] App. *Illyr.* 27; Suet. *Aug.* 20.
[13] Laharnar 2011.

38, in which his slingers proved highly effective against the Parthian mailed cavalry.[14] Antony himself, despite assembling an huge army for the same purpose in 36, was less successful, though his slingers proved their worth against mounted Parthian archers.[15] At the decisive encounter between Octavian and Antony at Actium off the west coast of Greece (Figure 23) in 31 BC, slingers and archers from Antony's army were embarked on his ships,[16] as they doubtless were on Octavian's too. Antony's legions are valuably documented by a series of coins issued in 32-31 BC (Figure 37). The battle is depicted on stone reliefs, wall paintings and ceramic lamps, but no slingers are, to my knowledge, featured.[17] A small number of stone *ballista* balls were plotted on the seabed offshore in 1993-97.[18]

---

[14] Dio 49.20.2.
[15] Dio 49.26.2.
[16] Dio 50.16.2, 18.6, 23.1.
[17] For example, Walker and Higgs 2001: nos 311, 314-315.
[18] See 'The Actium Project' (luna.cas.usf.edu/murray/Actium/brochur.html). Accessed 16 December 2022.

Chapter 8

Slingers under the Roman Empire

The many campaigns undertaken by the Roman army during the long reign of Augustus (27 BC-AD 14) lie outside the scope of this monograph. A few are illustrated by inscribed lead bullets, including the so-called 'Alpenfeldzug', undertaken in 16-15 BC by his stepsons Tiberius and Drusus.[1] Lead bullets of Augustan date have been recovered at legionary bases on the Rhine,[2] and eastwards from it along the River Lippe.[3] The reign witnessed numerous attacks on Iron Age hillforts, which have sometimes yielded bullets.[4]

Slingers and stone-throwers continued as an element in Roman forces under the Empire, participating in the wars of the Julio-Claudian period,[5] in the Jewish War of 66-73,[6] and in the civil wars of 68-70.[7] The inscribing of lead bullets is recorded up to Claudian times,[8] and uninscribed lead bullets are attested down to the Antonine Period and perhaps much later.[9] Bullets of baked clay and of stone continued in use.[10]

A slinger named Epitynchanus, on a gravestone at Rome which must date after AD 100,[11] is shown naked except for a short cloak wound round his right shoulder, a fold of which holds a supply of bullets (Figure 38).[12] The inscription, of which the first two letters are contained within the gable, reads: D M / EPITYNCHANO·FILI / ASTRO·M·ANTONIVS / HERMEROS·SVO ·B·M·F. *D(is) M(anibus) Epitynchano fili / astro M(arcus) Antonius / Hermeros suo b(ene)m(erenti) f(ecit)*. 'To the Spirits of the Departed and for Epitynchanus (my) stepson, Marcus Antonius Hermeros made (this) for him, well-deserving.' His civic status is not entirely clear. He was not a Roman citizen and

---

[1] Rageth, Zanier and Klein 2010; Martin-Kilcher 2011.
[2] Zandstra 2019 has details.
[3] Völling 1990: 49 nos 41-43, 47. At Haltern on the Lippe (no. 42), stone, clay and lead bullets have all been found, their number increased by recent finds.
[4] See, for example, Schlott 1999: 47, 79 Tafel 25, on the hillfort at Dünsberg north of Frankfurt; Peralta Labrador 2006 on the hillfort at La Loma, Spain.
[5] Tac. *Ann.* 2.20; 13.39. For the suggestion that slingers were among the forces available to Aulus Plautius at the time of the Claudian invasion of Britain in AD 43, see now Reid *et al.* 2022.
[6] Jos. *Bell. Jud.* 3.211 notes Syrian slingers and stone-throwers among the Roman forces.
[7] Tac. *Hist.* 2.22, 3.27, 3.31, 5.17.
[8] A bullet naming legion XIII found at the legionary fortress of Vindonissa (Windisch, Switzerland) must date to before c. AD 45 (Simonett 1947: 18 Abbildung 5). No inscribed bullets are as yet known from Britain, invaded in AD 43 under Claudius.
[9] Völling 1990: 35. Greep 1987 usefully discusses the evidence for slingers under the Empire.
[10] Vegetius (*De Re Mil*.1.16, 2.23), writing in the later 4th century AD, fails to mention either lead or clay bullets.
[11] The gravestone is set into the wall of the cloister of Santi Quattro Coronati on the Caelian Hill in Rome.
[12] De Minicis 1844: 11 tabula 1; *CIL* VI 17243; Stenhouse 2002: 204, no. 104; *Epigraphic Database Roma* no. 136197. The tombstone is less elongated than De Minicis depicts it.

Figure 38. Tombstone from Rome, naming the slinger Epitynchanus, AD 100 or later. After De Minicis, *Sulle antiche ghiande*, 1844, Roma: tabula 1.

Figure 39. Trajan's Column, Rome. A slinger and a stone-thrower. Photo: C. Cichorius, *Die Reliefs der Traiansäule*, 1896, Berlin: scene lxvi. Courtesy of Glasgow University Library.

probably of servile descent. The findspot in Rome suggests a slinger attached to one of the military formations stationed in the capital, but no such affiliation is indicated.

Slingers and stone-throwers are depicted in battle on Trajan's Column whose continuous frieze, carved c. AD 117, records the events of the emperor's two wars in Dacia, modern Romania, in 101-06 (Figures 39-41).[13] They are bearded, bare-headed, clad in Roman tunics, and have Roman hairstyles. Some are equipped with swords and small shields. Each wears a short cloak fastened at the right shoulder, a fold of which contains a supply of bullets. The spherical bullets look to be of stone, perhaps enlarged for the viewer's benefit. One slinger with his back to the viewer wields

[13] Cichorius 1896: scenes lxvi, lxx, lxxii, cxiii.

Figure 40. Trajan's Column, Rome. A stone-thrower poised to cast a stone. Photo: C. Cichorius, *Die Reliefs der Traiansäule*. 1896, Berlin: scene lxxii.
Courtesy of Glasgow University Library.

Figure 41. Trajan's Column, Rome. A slinger viewed from behind. Photo: C. Cichorius, *Die Reliefs der Traiansäule*, 1896, Berlin: scene cxiii. Courtesy of Glasgow University Library.

a smaller sling, perhaps for lead or clay bullets (Figure 41).[14] We have to allow for artistic licence as well as misunderstanding by the sculptors of the details of the military equipment. The slingers and stone-throwers are dressed not as tribesmen but as Romans.

Among the troops reviewed by Hadrian at Lambaesis, modern Algeria, in AD 128 were mounted slingers serving in a cohort of auxiliaries, the *cohors VI Commagenorum*, who shot stones from their slings.[15] On the Column of Marcus Aurelius at Rome, carved c. AD 180, elderly slingers, bearded and in heavy cloaks with bullets in their folds, may be Germanic (i.e. barbarian) slingers opposing Rome (Figure 42).[16] A likely weapons' store (*armamentarium*) at the legionary fortress at Lambaesis, Algeria, yielded a cache of about 6000 clay bullets and more than 300 stone bullets.[17] The dating is presumably in the Late Empire.

The homelands of slingers under the Empire are generally not specified. Nothing more is heard of Balearic slingers, though they continue to feature in Latin poetry.[18] Training programmes for slingers were instituted,[19] perhaps because specialised personnel, schooled from childhood, were no longer available. The training programmes also encompassed stone-throwing. Clearly those trained included legionaries, as bullets have been recovered at some of their fortresses. Even mounted horsemen could be slingers (see also above).[20]

Bodies of archers were transformed under the Empire into *cohortes sagittariae*, to be counted among the formally constituted *auxilia*; however, no specific units of slingers are attested before the Late Empire.[21] Perhaps slingers were sometimes 'bought in' for specific campaigns from communities well versed in slinging. Coulston has suggested that they doubled as *calones*, soldiers' servants;[22] but literary references to the latter do not hint at a fighting role.[23] No space is allocated to separate units of slingers in the Roman campaign-camp whose layout is described in the *De Munitionibus Castrorum*, a treatise dating the late 1st or early 2nd century AD.[24]

---

[14] Cichorius 1896: scene cxiii.
[15] *CIL* VIII 2532 = *ILS* 9134 = Smallwood 1966: no. 328.
[16] Petersen *et. al.* 1896: scene x. See Beckmann 2012: 144 figure 7.7.
[17] Völling 1990: 50 no. 73.
[18] E.g. Virg. *Aen*. 11. 580; Lucan *Phars*. 3.709-14; Sid. Apol. *Carm*. 23.345.
[19] Veg. *De Re Mil*. 2.23.
[20] Fougères 1896a: 1366 figure 3329.
[21] *Funditores* were among the forces available to the *magister militum per orientem* (military commander of troops in the East) in the Late Empire (*Not. Dig., Oriens* 7.16).
[22] Coulston 1988: vol. 1, 293.
[23] Speidel 2003; Thorburn 2003.
[24] Campbell 2018.

Figure 42. Column of Marcus Aurelius, Rome. A group of bearded slingers. Photo: E. Petersen, A. von Domaszewski and G. Calderini, *Die Marcus-Säule auf Piazza Colonna in Rom*, 1896, München: scene x. Courtesy of Glasgow University Library

The throwing of stones also continued, with slingers and stone-throwers sometimes acting in concert.[25] They are depicted together on Trajan's Column (Figure 39). Hand-sized stone balls, often described as '*ballista* balls', have been recovered at numerous military sites; it could be that many were meant to be hand-thrown.

[25] Tac. *Ann.* 2.20, 13.39.

Chapter 9

The role of slingers in battle and their effectiveness

The literary sources preserve accounts of slingers in battle, which allow us to assess their role. They did not operate in isolation but in conjunction with other light forces, most frequently with archers. Slingers were valued on the battlefield because of their range and accuracy. However, a lack of defensive armour meant they were vulnerable if confronted by heavily-armed and well-protected troops. At Pharsalus in 48 BC (above p. 41), when Pompey's cavalry fled the field, his archers and slingers, left exposed, were all cut down by Caesar's men.[1]

Slingers and archers were often deployed in the opening stages of a battle.[2] In his treatise entitled *The General*, the philosopher Onasander, writing in the mid-1st century AD,[3] placed archers and slingers in front of the phalanx (i.e. of the legions), which afforded the slingers sufficient space in which to whirl their slings and discharge the bullets.[4] Gaps in the phalanx allowed archers and slingers to retire before the main battle lines clashed.[5] They might then move to the wings and attack an enemy on its flank. In 36 BC Antony's javelin-men and slingers made a sally against the Parthians through the ranks of the legions.[6] Vegetius places slingers and an army's other light-armed troops behind the lines of legionaries, but when battle was joined, they emerged to engage the enemy.[7]

Sometimes slingers and archers are found positioned on the wings of an army,[8] or were intermingled with other troops.[9] Scenes on Trajan's Column show them and stone-throwers interspersed with legionaries and auxiliaries (Figures 39-40). The relief from Asculum depicts slingers standing in a single line (Figure 10).

What made slingers effective on a battlefield was their ability to strike accurately at a distance.[10] Dense showers of sling bullets, arrows and stones could disrupt an attack and even force an enemy to retreat.[11] In 206 BC the Carthaginian fleet was turned

---

[1] Caes. *BC* 3.93
[2] E.g. Polyb. 3.11.3; Onas. *Strat.* 20; App. *Hann.* 21.
[3] Smith 1998.
[4] Onas. *Strat.* 17.
[5] Onas. *Strat.* 19.
[6] Plut. *Ant.* 41.4.
[7] Veg. *De Re Mil.* 2.15.
[8] Caes. *BC* 3.88, *Bell. Afr.* 81, 83; Sall. *Jug.* 46.7, 100.2.
[9] Caes. *BG* 3.24, *BC* 1.83; Sall. *Jug.* 49.6; Front. *Strat.* 4.7.27; App. *BC* 2.75.
[10] Dio 49.20.2, 26.2.
[11] Caes. *B.Afr.* 83; Sall. *Jug.* 57; Diod. Sic. 5.18.3; Livy 36.18.3-5; Tac. *Ann.* 2.20.

away from Mallorca 'by a violent hailstorm of stone bullets'.[12] Accounts of slingers in battle give little support to the view that bullets were in fact shot in bulk from catapults.[13] Their ubiquitousness is in itself testimony to their effectiveness.

Distances of up to 350 m could be achieved, according to the skill of the slinger, the length of the sling-cords and the weight and type of the bullets.[14] Vegetius reports targets for archers and slingers set up during training at 600 Roman feet (180 m).[15] Lead bullets had a much higher velocity than clay or stone, and therefore a longer range. Slingers' ability to outrange archers, including the Parthian mounted archers, is emphasised.[16]

Their accuracy is repeatedly stressed.[17] Slingers were able, we are told, to bring down birds in flight,[18] so that pinpoint accuracy on a battlefield cannot cause surprise.[19] At a siege they could hit defenders on the battlements, even when shooting from ships.[20] The historian Claudius Quadrigarius, writing in the first century BC, observed that slingers at a siege of a town in Spain were at their most effective when aiming upwards at its defenders.[21] The concentration of bullets on the line of the hillfort ramparts at Burnswark, Dumfriesshire, attacked c. AD 142, demonstrates the accuracy of fire from the north rampart of the Roman camp at the foot of the hill, a distance of 150-180 m.[22] We have no information on whether or how the slingers and stone-throwers could be resupplied in battle; one option is that they retired from the fray once their supply had been expended.

Sling bullets were much feared for the serious wounds they could inflict, especially to the head.[23] Onasander describes sling bullets as the deadliest of the weaponry used by the light-armed.[24] They could bring sudden death without any spilling of blood.[25] Being hit by a sling bullet was excruciatingly painful. Helmeted legionaries with their

---

[12] Livy 28.37.
[13] As Rihll (2009: 160) proposed; rejected by Ma 2010; Campbell 2011: 692. The sling-stave (*fustibalus*) described by Vegetius (*De Re Mil.* 3.14) is not attested in the Late Republic.
[14] Technical aspects are addressed by Baatz 1990. See also Griffiths 1989: 261; Wild 1998: 299.
[15] Veg. 2.23.
[16] Xen. *Anab.* 3.4.16; Dio 49.26.2.
[17] Livy 38.29.7; Veg. *De Re Mil.* 1.16, 2.23.
[18] Virg. *Aen.* 11. 580; Sil. Ital. *Pun.* 8.521. See Fougères 1896a: 1366 figure 3329; Griffiths 1989: 263; Völling 1990: Abbildungen 17-18.
[19] Modern experiments have confirmed both range and accuracy. Videos available online illustrate the techniques of slinging.
[20] Diod. Sic. 5.18.3; Livy 24.34.
[21] Aul. Gell. *Noct. Att.* 9.1.1.
[22] Reid and Nicholson 2019: 468 figure 2.
[23] Livy 38.29. Rihll (2009: 163) downplays the efficacy of slinging.
[24] *Strat.* 19. For counter-measures adopted by soldiers at Dyrrhachium in 48 BC see above p. 41.
[25] Diod. Sic. 19.109; Veg. *De Re Mil.* 1 16; Amm. Marc. 31.7.

large shields enjoyed some protection against bullets; the slingers themselves had none.[26] Bullets could crush shields, helmets and body armour.[27]

We hear of injuries caused to senior commanders. Leosthenes, an Athenian general at Lamia in 323 BC, was struck on the head by a bullet; carried back to camp unconscious, he died three days later.[28] At Cannae in 216, the consul L. Aemilius Paulus was severely wounded by a bullet in the opening phase of the battle.[29] At Thermopylae in 191 BC the Seleucid King Antiochus III was hit in the mouth by a sling stone which knocked his teeth out.[30] In 54 BC Caesar's legate Aurunculeius Cotta was struck full-in-the-face by a bullet,[31] which was probably of baked clay; he was able to continue but was killed shortly after. During the Jewish War of AD 66-73 King Herod Agrippa was wounded in the elbow by a sling stone.[32] At the siege of Jerusalem in AD 70 the historian Josephus was struck on the head by a stone which briefly knocked him unconscious.[33] Doubtless many soldiers in the ranks were hit too, but their fate did not merit individualised recording. A lead bullet found in a burial at Vergina, Macedonia, lodged in a skeleton's ribs, was presumably fatal.[34]

The medical writer Celsus, writing in the mid-1st century AD, reports on the wounds caused by stone pebbles and lead bullets embedded in the body. A doctor needed to know how to extract them from flesh, from bone and from joints.[35] The historian Livy reports the behaviour of Galatian warriors, writhing on the ground, at a battle against the Romans in Asia Minor in 189 BC when hit by bullets they did not know how to extract.[36]

According to Onasander, bullets heated by passage through the air penetrated the skin more easily, which quickly closed over the wound.[37] The story of the Biblical David may be taken up again. 'David put his hand in his bag, and took thence a stone, and slang it, and smote the Philistine in his forehead, that the stone sunk into his forehead; and he fell upon his face to the earth'.[38]

---

[26] For bullets sounding against shields, see Xen. *Anab.* 4.3.29.
[27] Diod. Sic. 5.18.3.
[28] Diod. Sic. 18.13.5.
[29] Livy 22.49.1.
[30] Plut. *Cato Major* 14.1.
[31] Caes. *BG* 5.35.
[32] Jos. *Bell. Jud.* 4.11.
[33] Jos. *Bell. Jud.* 5.541.
[34] Hood 1961: 19.
[35] *De Med.* 7.5.4. Medical aspects are discussed by Moog 2002.
[36] Livy 38.21.11. The slingers were Cretans.
[37] *Strat.* 19. Confirmed to me by Dr J.H. Reid.
[38] *I Samuel* 17.49 (King James Version).

Chapter 10

Conclusion

The foregoing pages have reviewed several thousand surviving sling bullets from more than 70 sites and locations, some known since the nineteenth century and first published in Latin; subsequent discoveries have been published in Spanish, Catalan, Portuguese, Italian, French, German and English. Recent decades have seen an enormous expansion of the corpus of sling bullets, from an increasing number of locations, well beyond the finds made long ago at Asculum (Ascoli) and Perusia (Perugia). Fieldwork and surface survey in several countries have yielded much new information.

Some parts of the Roman world are well represented in the archaeological record, others not at all. Slingers may be mentioned in the literary accounts of a campaign, battle or siege, where no bullets have as yet been forthcoming. Conversely, bullets have been discovered at battle-sites where the literary sources fail to report the presence of slingers.

In periods of civil war the total number of Roman legions in commission grew dramatically.[1] The numbers of light-armed troops including cavalry, slingers and archers must have increased too,[2] as the armies led by the various protagonists grew in strength; but for the most part we lack precise information.

Literary accounts of slingers record that the Roman army on campaign outside Italy generally resorted to locally-recruited slingers.[3] But allied communities in Italy also furnished the Romans with slingers, down to the Social War and probably later. The poet Silius Italicus, writing in the 1st century AD, records, among the many Italian contingents in the Roman army against Hannibal at Cannae in 216 BC, slingers from Central Italy.[4] At the siege of Asculum in 90-89 slingers from the towns of Opitergium and Firmum were present, and the defenders of Asculum deployed slingers too (above p. 18). Sulla's army at Pompeii in 89 BC included slingers of unknown ethnicity (above p. 23). Large numbers of clay bullets found in a single deposit at the old Latin Colony of Paestum (above p. 23) indicate their continued use. The slingers in Pompey's army at Brundisium in 49 BC and in Caesar's army at Dyrrhachium in 48 could well have been recruited in Italy rather than east of the Adriatic (above pp. 35, 41). Equally, we

---

[1] Schmitthenner 1958; Brunt 1971: 473.
[2] Cheesman 1914: 11; Saddington 1982: 5.
[3] Völling 1990: 55 Liste 3 gathers the available evidence.
[4] Sil. Ital. *Pun.* 8.519-22.

cannot be sure that some of the slingers defending the town of Perusia in 41 BC were not of local origin, who had practised slinging in their youth.

How bodies of slingers were organised and commanded largely eludes us. Pompey in 49-48 BC could muster two cohorts of slingers, each of 600 men.[5] It is tempting to equate these with the slingers we know he acquired from Crete and from Thrace.[6] Bodies of slingers could be numbered in thousands.[7] In battle they were usually deployed, so far as we can determine, as a single group.[8]

Finds of sling bullets add to our knowledge of battles in this period, hint at encounters not otherwise reported, and identify lines of march. In particular they have allowed the localising of the battlefield at Munda in 45 BC (above, p. 44). The burgeoning field of 'battlefield archaeology' seems likely to improve our appreciation.[9] Sometimes only the discovery of bullets demonstrates the presence of slingers, e.g. at Numantia in 133 BC, at Asculum in 90-89 or at Pompeii in 89. Slingers could find themselves ranged on opposite sides at a battle. Despite their hard-earned skills, slingers always came low in the army's pecking-order.[10] Slingers and archers were regularly embarked on warships when sea battles were imminent (above pp. 31, 42, 65), along with bodies of legionaries.[11]

Bullets can name commanders, sometimes confirming literary sources (e.g. the presence of Octavian's legate Q. Salvidienus Rufus at the siege of Perusia); they also bring before us otherwise unknown military tribunes and centurions, whose service is thus closely datable. Generally Roman names inscribed on lead bullets are given in the form *praenomen* followed by *nomen* (e.g. Gaius Varius); *cognomina* (surnames) were not yet in common use by most Romans. *Scaeva* (Figure 32.8) seems to be the only *cognomen* securely attested on a bullet naming an individual soldier.[12]

Legions are named on sling bullets. Is this evidence that legionaries actually shot them? Bodies of slingers were marshalled on the battlefield quite separately from legions and needed space to shoot not available to the heavily armed legionaries standing close together in line, so that we could be drawn to the view that centurions named on bullets at Perusia and elsewhere merely supervised the casting process, before distributing the resulting bullets to non-Roman slingers. To explain the naming

---

[5] Caes. *BC* 3.4.
[6] App. *BC* 2.49, 71.
[7] See Pritchett 1992: 63.
[8] For an exception, at Numantia, see above p. 12.
[9] Exemplified by the battle at Baecula (207 BC), on which see Bellón *et al.* 2009; Quesada Sanz *et al.* 2015; Bellón Ruiz *et al.* 2017; Marcos Carreras 2017: figure 41-43. On the battle at Monte Bernorio during Augustus' Cantabrian Wars, see Fernández-Götz *et al.* 2018.
[10] Slinging was the 'cheapest of the military skills' (Pritchett 1991: 53).
[11] Pritchett 1991: 60.
[12] He is named in later authors as 'Cassius Scaeva' (Plut. *Caes.* 16; Suet. *Caes.* 68; Val. Max. 3.2.23) but simply as 'Scaeva' in contemporary sources (Caes. *BC* 3.53; Cic. *Att.* 14.10).

of individual legions on bullets, Völling suggested that bodies of slingers were at this time closely associated with particular Roman legions.[13] Another possibility could be that soldiers' servants made the bullets.

If individual legions prepared and shot their own bullets, we could look for distinctions in shape and weight. At Perusia, for example, bullets shot by legion IV differ from those naming legion VI.[14] The various abbreviations of the name Apidius, chief centurion of legion VI, could suggest familiarity with him as an individual. Inscribed lead bullets naming legions are reported from the battlefields of Munda (45 BC) and Mutina (43 BC). Interestingly, the literary sources fail to mention contingents of slingers as present at either battle.

Significant concentrations of inscribed bullets naming legions come from sieges. At Perusia, where surviving bullets demonstrate that slingers were active on both sides (above, p. 54), it seems unlikely that either Lucius Antonius or Octavian had had the opportunity to recruit specialist contingents before the siege began. While battles generally lasted a single day, sieges could endure for months; the legionaries were not arrayed in a battle-line and should have had time to prepare and use bullets. I conclude that bullets naming particular legions were indeed made and shot by them. Völling identified six Types among surviving lead bullets at both Asculum and Perusia.[15] We could wonder therefore whether some Types are to be ascribed to the besiegers and some to the defenders of these towns, but no such distinction seems evident; bullets shot by the opposing sides are distinguishable by their inscriptions. Perhaps isotope analysis in future will help to clarify the sources of the lead; soldiers trapped inside Asculum and Perusia may well have melted down whatever lead artefacts were available.[16]

Slingers from the Balearic Islands were long held in high regard (above p. 10). We could therefore expect their widespread employment in the civil wars. They are attested among Caesar's forces in 53 BC but are not named thereafter.[17] The populations of the Islands were perhaps by now depleted.[18] Can they be identified from the bullets they customarily used? Large numbers of bullets have been found on Menorca and on Ibiza, where presumably they had been made (above pp. 8, 10). Future study of Balearic bullets, especially by lead isotope analysis, could lead to their identification at other sites. Slingers attested in the East were often drawn from local kingdoms and tribes.

---

[13] Völling 1990: 46.
[14] Benedetti 2012a: nos 15-16, 17-22.
[15] Völling 1990: 54 nos 102, 122.
[16] The lead of one bullet from Asculum, inscribed FIR (above, p. 18), may have originated in Tuscany (Müller *et al.* 2014).
[17] The poet Lucan features a Balearic slinger at a naval battle off Massilia (Marseille) in 49 BC (above p. 35).
[18] Zucca 1998: 101, 189.

Enormous numbers of bullets must have been produced, of which we now have only a tiny percentage.[19] Sometimes they are found in large groups, which may represent quantities prepared but never used (above pp. 23, 27). Some sites have yielded both stone and clay bullets, and sometimes lead, clay and stone, which could indicate the presence of different groups of slingers.[20] Sling bullets are the most prolific category of Roman weaponry to survive from antiquity, more than arrowheads, spearheads and javelins, which could be recovered and sometimes shot back.[21]

The surviving testimony from Perusia (above p. 53) could suggest that all or almost all lead sling bullets were inscribed. This would be misleading. It may be suspected that inscribed bullets at Perusia were the only ones retained by local collectors. At Asculum (above p. 15) only a small minority were inscribed. At some sites none of the bullets bore inscriptions. Sometimes all the slingers in a contingent appear to have used the same text, for example the *Opitergini* and *Firmani* at Asculum or the Aetolians at Numantia; at other times a variety of wording is found, naming, it may be, the commander, a tribune or a centurion.

The impact of bullets was psychological and propagandist as well as physical. Their sound in flight could disconcert the opposing troops (above p. 8). Where bullets were picked up on the ground and read by the opposing side, they identified the attackers, whose messages were often intended to undermine morale, with a mixture of threats and insults, some sexual.[22] With the publication of more graffiti from Pompeii and Herculaneum, the testimony from Perusia can be seen in context.[23] Inscriptions incised on *ballista* balls (above p. 26) are similarly contemporary. The targets of such taunts were generally the opposing commanders rather than the soldiers. Some commanders are reported on inscribed bullets, e.g. Sertorius, Agrippa, Octavian and Antony. Others such as Sulla, Caesar (except as a target), Pompey the Great, and Augustus and his stepsons, are not named. Writing messages on projectiles has been popular through the ages.[24] The inscriptions on bullets and *ballista* balls were not intended to be symbolic. They could be picked up and read.

The urge to inscribe bullets in the first century BC can, at least in part, be linked to the circumstances of civil war when the inscriptions could be read and understood by both sides. It is less common to find inscribed bullets directed at non-Latin readers.

---

[19] One bullet, now lost, includes the text X MILIA, which it is easiest to suppose, with Mommsen, was in origin an instruction '(Make) ten thousand'. The origin of this bullet is uncertain; Zangemeister tentatively assigned it to Perusia (1885: no. 112).
[20] Above, pp. 2, 26, 66.
[21] Xen. *Anab.* 3.4.17; Polyb. 6.22; Sall. *Jug.* 58; Livy 10.29. Though modern experiments have shown that bullets landing on soft ground could sink out of sight and be difficult to retrieve (information from Dr. J.H. Reid), some were clearly picked up and read (above pp. 23, 44).
[22] Olson 2008. For the songs sung by his soldiers at Caesar's Triumph in 46 BC see Suet. *Caes.* 49.
[23] See now *The Ancient Graffiti Project* (https://ancientgraffiti.org), directed by Prof. Rebecca Benefiel.
[24] Kelly 2012 cites modern parallels.

Conclusion

We can sometimes detect, in the wording, the usages of everyday speech.[25] There are examples of soldiers' coarse humour (above pp. 49, 59). As the bullets were contemporary with the historical events they illustrate, the style of lettering and the phraseology are closely datable.

This is an ever-growing but under-appreciated resource. As Jerzy Linderski once remarked, 'Military historians should read their slingshots'.[26] Future discoveries of bullets will surely bring more surprises and add to our knowledge of military events in the Late Republic.

---

[25] E.g. *ILLRP* 1099 (*tibe* for *tibi*), 1111 (*Caesarus* for *Caesaris*); Benedetti 2012a: no. 33 (*esureis* for *esurieis*).
[26] Linderski 1998: 471.

Reference 1

Glossary

Castellum	Roman fort
Centurio (centurion)	Commander of a century of 80 men in a legion.
Cognomen	Roman surname, e.g. Caesar.
Cohors (cohort)	Component part of a legion, usually of 500-600 men.
Consul	Supreme magistrate at Rome, one of two elected annually, who took charge of the army on campaign.
Funditor (plural *funditores*)	Slinger
Glans (plural *glandes*)	Sling bullet
Imperator	Victorious commander of a Roman army.
Interpunct	Medial dot marking the division between words in a Latin inscription.
Legatus (legate)	Senatorial officer to whom a magistrate on campaign delegated part of his administrative, juridical or military duties; later, commander of a legion.
Nomen	Roman family name, e.g. Julius.
Praenomen	Roman first name, e.g. Gaius.
Praetor	Senatorial magistrate at Rome, second in rank only to a consul.
Primus pilus	Chief centurion of a legion.
Propraetor	Governor of a province who was previously a *praetor* at Rome.
Proconsul	Governor of a province who was previously a *consul* at Rome.
Quaestor	Senatorial magistrate at Rome, with financial responsibilities.
Tribunus militum	Middle-ranking officer in a legion.
Triumvir rei publicae constituendae	Member of the Commission of Three, for ordering the state

Reference 2

Bibliography

Epigraphic corpora

AE *l'Année* Épigraphique, 1889-. Paris: Presses universitaires de France.
CIL *Corpus Inscriptionum Latinarum*, 1862-. Berlin: Reimer.
ILLRP *Inscriptiones Latinae Liberae Rei Publicae*, 1957-63, ed. A. Degrassi. Firenze: La Nuova Italia.
ILS *Inscriptiones Latinae Selectae*, 1892-1906, ed. H. Dessau. Berlin: Weidman.
SEG *Supplementum Epigraphicum Graecum* 1923-, Leiden / Boston: Brill.

References

Adams, J.N. 1982. *The Latin Sexual Vocabulary*. London: Duckworth.
Alföldy, G. 1975. *Die römischen Inschriften von Tarraco*. Band 1 (Madrider Forschungen 10). Berlin: De Gruyter.
Amela Valverde, L. 2015. La batalla de Andagoste. *Panta Rei. Revista digital de Ciencia y Didáctica de la Historia* 9: 51-61.
Baatz, D. 1990. Schleudergeshosse aus Blei. Eine waffentechnische Untersuchung. *Saalburg Jahrbuch* 45: 59-67 = D. Baatz, *Bauten und Katapulte des römischen Heeres* (Mavors 11), 1994: 294-302. Stuttgart: Steiner.
Bauchhenss, G. 1978. *Corpus Signorum Imperii Romani. Deutschland, Band III.1. Germania Inferior I. Bonn und Umgebung. Die militärischen Grabendenkmäler*. Bonn: Habelt.
Bechtold, B., Frey-Kupper, S., Madella, M. and Brugnone, A. 1999. *La necropoli di Lilybaeum*. Roma: L'Erma di Bretschneider.
Beckmann, M. 2012. *The Column of Marcus Aurelius. The Genesis and Meaning of a Roman Imperial Monument*. Chapel Hill: University of North Carolina Press.
Bellón, J.P., Gómez Cabeza, F., Ruiz, A., Molinos, M., Sánchez, A., Gutiérrez, L., Rueda, C. Martínez, A.L., Ortega, C., Lozano, G. and Fernández, R. 2009. Baecula. An archaeological analysis of the location of a battle of the Second Punic War, in Á. Morillo, N. Hanel and E. Martín (eds) *Limes XX. Estudios sobre la frontera romana* (Anejos de Gladius 13): 253-65. Madrid: Ediciones Polifemo.
Bellón Ruiz, J.P., Rueda Galán, C., Lechuga Chica, M.Á., Ruiz Rodríguez, A. and Molinos Molinos, A. 2017. Archaeological methodology applied to the analysis of battlefields and military camps of the Second Punic War: Baecula. *Quaternary International* 435: 81-97.
Beltrán Lloris, F. 1990. La 'pietas' de Sertorio. *Gerión* 8: 211-26.
Beltrán Lloris, M. 2016. Una glans inscripta del Museo de Zaragoza, in *Homenaje a la profesora Concepción Blasco Bosqued* (Anejos a Cuadernos de Preistoria y Arqueología 2): 275-80. Madrid: Universidad Autónoma de Madrid.
Benedetti, L. 2012a. *Glandes Perusinae. Revisione e aggiornamenti*. Roma: Quasar.

Benedetti, L. 2012b. Proettili da fionda in piombo iscritti, in R. Friggeri, M.G. Cecere Granino and G.L. Gregori (eds), *Terme di Diocleziano, la collezione epigrafica*: 375-86. Milano: Electa.

Bishop, M.C. and Coulston, J.C.N. 2006. *Roman Military Equipment, from the Punic Wars to the Fall of Rome*. Second edition. Oxford: Oxbow.

Blanco Freijeiro, A. 1983. Ategua. *Noticiario Arqueológico Hispánico* 15: 93-136.

Ble Gimeno, E. 2016. *Guerra y conflicto en el nordeste de Hispania durante el periodo romano republicano (218-45 a.C.)*. Unpublished Ph.D. dissertation, Universitat de Barcelona.

Bode, M., Hanel, N. and Rothenhöfer, P. 2021. Roman lead ingots from Macedonia. The Augustan shipwreck of Comacchio (prov. Ferrara, Italy) and the reinterpretation of its lead ingots. Provenance deductions from isotope analysis. *Archaeological and Anthropological Science* 13: 163.

Bosman, A.V.A.J. 1995. Pouring lead in the pouring rain. Making lead slingshot under battle conditions. *Journal of Roman Military Equipment Studies* 6: 99-103.

Botermann, H. 1969. *Die Soldaten und die römische Politik in der Zeit von Caesars Tod bis zum Begründung des Zweiten Triumvirats* (Zetemata 46). München: Beck.

Broughton, T.R.S. 1951. *The Magistrates of the Roman Republic*, volume 2. New York: American Philological Association.

Brouquier-Reddé, V. 1997. L'équipement militaire d'Alésia d'après les nouvelles recherches (prospections et fouilles). *Journal of Roman Military Equipment Studies* 8: 276-88.

Brulet, R. and Lepot, A. 2018. *Glandes plumbae*. Une balle de fronde inscrite découverte en Belgique. *Signa* 7: 290-33.

Brunt, P.A. 1971. *Italian Manpower 225 B.C.- A.D. 14*. Oxford: Clarendon Press.

Buoncore, M. 1989. Rhegium Iulium. *Supplementa Italica* 5: 29-84.

Buonopane, A. 2014. Due ghiande missili col nome del fabbricante nel Museo Archeologico al Teatro Romano di Verona, in M. Chiabà (ed.), *Hoc quoque laboris praemium. Scritti in onore di Gino Bandelli*: 19-32. Trieste: Università di Trieste.

Burns, M. 2004. Pompeii under siege. A missile assemblage from the Social War. *Journal of Roman Military Equipment Studies* 14/15 (2003-2004): 1-9.

Butera, C.J. and Sears, M.A. 2017. The camps of Brutus and Cassius at Philippi, 42 BC. *Hesperia* 86: 359-77.

Callu, J.-P., Morel, J.-P., Rebuffat, R., and Hallier, G. 1965 *Thamusida. Fouilles du service des antiquités de Maroc*. Tome 1. Paris.

Cameron, J. 1934. *The Skeleton of British Neolithic Man*. London: Williams and Norgate.

Campbell, D.B. 2005. *Siege Warfare in the Roman World, 146 BC – AD 378*. Oxford: Osprey.

Campbell, D.B. 2011. Ancient catapults. Some hypotheses re-examined. *Hesperia* 80: 677-700.

Campbell, D.B. 2018. *Fortifying a Roman Camp. The Liber de Munitionibus Castrorum*. Glasgow: Bocca della Verità Publishing.

Chabot, L. and Feugère, M. 1993. Les armes de l'oppidum de La Cloche (Les Pennes-Mirabeau, B.-du-Rh.) et la destruction du site au 1er siècle avant notre ère. *Documents d'Archéologie Méridionale* 16: 337-51.

Chatelain, L. 1942. Une communication sur les balles de fronde de Volubilis. *Bulletin archéologique du comité des travaux historiques et scientifiques* 1941-1942: 400-01.

Cheesman, G.L. 1914 *The Auxilia of the Roman Imperial Army*. Oxford: Clarendon Press.

Cichorius, C. 1896. *Die Reliefs der Traiansäule*. Berlin: Reimer.

Contreras Rodrigo, F., Müller, R. and Valle de Tarazaga, F.J. 2006. El asentamiento militar romano de Sanitja (123-45 a.C.). Una aproximación a su contexto histórico. *Mayurka* 31: 233-49.

Corzo Sánchez, R. 1977. *Osuna de Pompeyo a César: Excavaciónes en la muralla republicana.* Sevilla: Universidad de Sevilla.

Corzo Sánchez, R. 1986. Luftbilder römischen Lager aus republikanischer Zeit in Spanien. Die belagerung von Ategua durch Julius Caesar (45 v.Chr.), in C. Unz (ed.), *Studien zu den Militärgrenzen Roms III*: 689-91. Stuttgart: Theiss.

Costabile, F. 1985. Salvidieno Rufo e la *legio X Fretensis* nella guerra navali fra Ottaviano e Sesto Pompeio, 42-36 a.c. *Rivista Storica Calabrese* 6: 357-74.

Coulston, J.C.N. 1988. *Trajan's Column. The Sculpting and Relief Content of a Roman Propaganda Monument.* Unpublished PhD dissertation, University of Newcastle.

Crawford, M.H. 1974. *Roman Republican Coinage.* Cambridge: Cambridge University Press.

Dart, C.J. 2014. *The Social War 91-88 BCE. A History of the Italian Insurgency against the Roman Republic.* London: Ashgate.

De Castro Nunes, J., Fabião, C. and Guerra, A. 1988. *O acampamento militar romano de Lomba do Canho (Arganil).* Arganil: Museu Regional de Arqueologia.

D'Ercole, V. and Savi, F. 2017. Le armi dei Romani dal Modenese, in L. Malnati, S. Pellegrini, F. Piccinini and C. Stefani (eds) *Mutina Splendidissima. La città romana e la sua eredità*: 366-69. Roma: De Luca.

De Minicis, G. 1844. *Sulle antiche ghiande missili e sulle loro iscrizioni.* Roma: Tipi della reverenda camera apostolica.

De Nicolás Mascaró, J.C. 1983. Romanización de Menorca, in *Geografie e Historia de Ciutadella de Menorca.* Menorca: Museo Arqueológico de Ibiza y Formentera.

Deyber, A. 1994 Projectiles, armes inertes, in M.-C. Bianchini (ed.) *Vercingétorix et Alésia*: 267-68. Paris: Réunion des Musées nationaux.

Deyber, A. and Luginbühl, T. 2018. *Cimbri* and *Teutones* against Rome. First research results concerning the battle of *Arausio* (105 BC), in M. Fernández-Götz and N. Roymans (eds) *Conflict Archaeology. The Materialities of collective Violence from Prehistory to Late Antiquity*: 155-66. London: Routledge.

Díaz Ariño, B. 2005. Glandes inscriptae de la Península Ibérica. *Zeitschrift für Papyrologie und Epigraphik* 153: 219-36.

Díaz Ariño, B. 2008. *Epigrafía Latina Republicana de Hispania.* Barcelona: Universitet de Barcelona.

Domergue, C. 1970. Un témoignage sur l'industrie minière et metallurgique du plomb dans la region d'Azuaga (Badajoz) pendant la guerre de Sertorius, in *XI Congreso Arqueológico Nacional, Mérida 1968*: 608-26. Zaragoza: Universidad secretaria general de los congresos arquelógicos nacionales.

Domínguez Monedero, A.J. 2005. Los mercenarios baleáricos, in B. Costa and J.H. Fernández (eds), *Guerra y ejército en el mundo Fenicio-Púnico*: 163-89. Ibiza: Museo Arqueológico de Ibiza y Formentera.

Doyen, J.-M. 2011. Les monnaies d'Ebusus en Gaule du Nord et en Bretagne. Un faux 'traceur' des campagnes césariennes? *Revue Numismatique* 167: 26-83.

Durán Recio, V. 2002. *La batalla de Munda.* Écija: Artes gráficas Serrano.

Engel, A. and Paris, P. 1906. *Une forteresse ibérique à Osuna.* Paris: Imprimerie nationale.

Fernández Gómez, F. 2009. La colección de glandes con marcas en el Museo Arqueológico de Sevilla, in *Espacios, usos y formas de la epigrafía Hispana en épocas antigua y tardoantigua: homenaje al Dr Armin U. Stylow*: 145-56. Mérida: Instituto de Arqueología.

Fernández-Götz, M., Torres-Martínez, J.F. and Martínez-Velasco, A. 2018. The battle at Monte Bernorio and the Augustan conquest of Cantabrian Spain, in M. Fernández-Götz and N. Roymans (eds) *Conflict Archaeology. The Materialities of collective Violence from Prehistory to Late Antiquity*:127-40. London: Routledge.

Ferreiro López, M.A. 2005. Munda, in J.F. Rodriguez Neila, E. Melchor Gil and J. Mellado Rodriguez (eds) *Julio César y Corduba. Tiempo y espacio en la campaña de Munda, 49-45 a.C.*: 383-98. Córdoba: Fundación Prasa.

Feugère M. 2002. *Weapons of the Romans*. Stroud: Tempus.

Feugère, M. 2008. Une balle de fronde du centurion C. Varius à Saint-Pargoire (Hérault). *Instrumentum* 28: 16-17.

Feugère, M., Gagnol, M., and Buffat, L. 2020. The nature and dating of Republican camps at Lautagne (Valence) through the small finds. *Journal of Roman Archaeology* 33: 331-40.

Fields, N. 2018. *Mutina 43 BC. Mark Antony's Struggle for Survival*. Oxford: Osprey.

Fogolari, G. and Scarfì, B.M. 1970. *Adria Antica*. Venezia: Alfieri.

Fontenla Ballesta, S. 2005. Glandes de honda procedentes de la batalla de Asso. *Alberca* [Revista de la Asociación de Amigos del Museo Arqueológico de Lorca] 3: 67-84.

Fortnum, C.D.E. 1864. 14 May, 1863. *Proceedings of the Society of Antiquaries of London*, series 2, volume 2: 268-70.

Fortnum, C.D.E. 1870. 29 April 1869. *Proceedings of the Society of Antiquaries of London*, series 2, volume 4: 313-16.

Foss, C. 1975. A bullet of Tissaphernes. *Journal of Hellenic Studies* 95: 25-30.

Fougères, G. 1896a. Funda, in C.V. Daremberg and E. Saglio (eds) *Dictionnaire des antiquités grecques et romaines*, tome 2: 1363-66. Paris: Hachette.

Fougères, G. 1896b. Glans, in C.V. Daremberg and E. Saglio (eds), *Dictionnaire des antiquités grecques et romaines*, tome 2: 1608-11. Paris: Hachette.

Gabba, E. 1971. The Perusine war and Triumviral Italy. *Harvard Studies in Classical Philology* 75: 139-60.

Gabba, E. 1994. Rome and Italy. The Social War, in J.A. Crook, A. Lintott and E. Rawson (eds) *The last Age of the Roman Republic, 146-43 BC* (Cambridge Ancient History 9): 104-28.

Gabrielli, G. 1885. Ascoli Piceno. *Notizie degli Scavi di Antichitá* 1885: 429-30.

Gabrielli, G. and Zangemeister, K.F. 1877. Scavi per ghiande missili eseguiti in Ascoli Piceno. *Bullettino dell'instituto di corrispondenza archeologica* 9: 17-76.

Garcia Garrido, M. and Lalana, L. 1993. Algunos glandes de plomo con inscripciones latinas y púnicas hallados en Hispania. *Acta Numismatica* 21-23 (1991-93), 101-07.

Garcia González, J. 2017. *Las glandes inscriptae come vehículos de propaganda política en Roma. El caso del bellum Sertorianum*. Unpublished MA dissertation, Universidad de Madrid.

Garcia González, J. 2019. Quintus Sertorius pro consule. Connotaciones de la magistratura proconsular afirmada en las *glandes inscriptae Sertorianae*. *Anas* 25-26: 189-206.

Goldsworthy, A. 2006 *Caesar. Life of a Colossus*. New Haven and London: Yale University Press.

Gomes, S.S., Araújo, M.F., Monge Soares, A.M. and Correia, V.H. 2017. Provenance evidence for Roman lead artefacts of distinct chronology from Portuguese archaeological sites. *Journal of Archaeological Science Reports* 16: 149-56.

Gómez-Pantoja, J.L. and Morales Hernández, F. 2002. Sertorio en Numancia. Una nota sobre los campamentos de la Gran Atalaya, in Á. Morillo (ed), *Arqueología militar romana en Hispania* (Gladius Anejos 5), 303-310. Madrid.

Gómez-Pantoja, J.L. and Morales Hernández, F. 2008. Los etolios en Numancia. *Saldvie* 8: 37-58.

González, J. 1996. P. Cornelius Scipio Aemilianus et Aetoli. *Athenaeum* 84: 143-56.

Granger-Taylor, H. 2012. Fragments of linen from Masada, Israel, in M.L. Nosch and H. Koefoed (eds) *Wearing the Cloak. Dressing the Soldier in Roman Times* (Ancient Textiles 10): 56-84. Oxford: Oxbow.

Greco, E. and Theodorescu, D. 1980. *Poseidonia-Paestum*, volume 1, *La 'Curia'*. Roma: École française de Rome.

Greep, S. 1987. Lead sling-shot from Windridge Farm, St Albans and the use of the sling by the Roman army in Britain. *Britannia* 18: 185-200.

Griffiths, W.B. 1989. The sling and its place in the Roman imperial army, in C. van Driel-Murray (ed.) *Roman Military Equipment. The Sources of Evidence* (BAR international series 476): 255-79. Oxford: British Archaeological Reports.

Griffiths, W.B. 1992. The hand-thrown stone. *Arbeia Journal* 2: 1-11.

Griffiths, W.B. and Carrick, P. 1994. Reconstructing Roman slings. *Arbeia Journal* 3: 1-11.

Gruat, P. 2006. Découverte de trois nouvelles balles de fronde en plomb de l'armée romaine. *Les Cahiers d'Archéologie Aveyronnaise* 19: 111-15.

Gruat, P., Marty, G. and Poujol, J. 2002. Des balles de fronde en plomb de l'armée romaine à Caylus / Puech Boussac (Saint-Affrique). *Les Cahiers d'Archéologie Aveyronnaise* 16: 87-96.

Grünewald, M. and Richter, A. 2006. Zeugen Caesars Schwerster Schlacht? Beschriftete andalusische Schleuderblei aus der Zeit des Zweiten Punischen Krieges und der Kampagne von Munda. *Zeitschrift für Papyrologie und Epigraphik* 157: 261-69.

Grünewald, M. and Richter, A. 2009. Zeugen Caesars Schwerster Schlacht? Beschriftete andalusische Schleuderblei aus der Zeit des Zweiten Punischen Krieges und der Kampagne von Munda, in Á. Morillo, N. Hanel and E. Martín (eds) *Limes XX. Estudios sobre la frontera romana* (Anejos de Gladius 13): 445-56. Madrid: Ediciones Polifemo.

Guarducci, M. 1939. *Inscriptiones Creticae II. Tituli Cretae Occidentalis*. Roma: Libreria dello Stato.

Guerra, A. 1987. Acerca dos projécteis para funda da Lomba do Canho (Arganil). *O Arqueólogo Português*, série 4.5: 161-77.

Hallett, J.P. 1977. Perusinae glandes and the changing image of Augustus. *American Journal of Ancient History* 2: 151-71.

Harmand, J. 1967. *L'armée et le soldat à Rome de 107 à 50 avant notre ère*. Paris: Picard.

Henry, B.M. 1972. *La fronde en Italie du VIIè siècle avant J.-C. à l'Empire Romain*. Unpublished diplome de l'École Pratique des Hautes Études. Paris.

Henry, B.M. 1974. L'emploi du terme 'legio' sur les projectiles de fronde romains et l'évolution sociale de l'Italie antique. *Caesarodunum* 9: 226-31.

Herbig, R. 1952 *Die jüngeretruskischen Steinsarkophage* (Die antiken Sarkophagreliefs 7). Berlin: Mann.

Hömke, N. 2010 Bit by bit towards death. Lucan's Scaeva and the aesthetisization of dying, in N. Hömke (ed.) *Lucan's bellum civile. Between Epic Translation and aesthetic Innovation*: 91-104. Berlin / New York: De Gruyter.

Hood, M.S.F. 1961. *Archaeology in Greece 1960-61*. London: Society for the Promotion of Hellenic Studies.

Jones, R. and Robinson, D. 2004. The making of an élite house. The House of the Vestals at Pompeii. *Journal of Roman Archaeology* 17: 107-30.

Kelly, A. 2012. The Cretan slinger at war. A weighty exchange. *Annual of the British School at Athens* 107: 273-311.

Keppie, L. 1983. *Colonisation and veteran Settlement in Italy, 47-14 BC*. London: British School at Rome.

Keppie, L. 1984. *The Making of the Roman Army. From Republic to Empire*. London: Batsford.

Keppie, L. 2000. *Legions and Veterans. Roman Army Papers, 1971-2000*. Stuttgart: Steiner.

Keppie, L. 2022. Consular legions in the Late Republic, in F. Santangelo, W. Eck and K. Vössing (eds) *Emperor, Army and Society. Studies of Roman Imperial History for Anthony R. Birley*: 187-98. Bonn: Habelt.

Korfmann, M. 1973. The sling as a weapon. *Scientific American* 229/4: 34-42.

Kraay, C.M. and Hirmer, M. 1966. *Greek Coins*. London: Thames and Hudson.

Kromayer, J. 1897. Entwicklung der römischen Flotte vom Seeräuberkriege des Pompeius bis zur Schlacht von Actium. *Philologus* 56: 426-91.

Kromayer, J. and Veith, G. 1922-29. *Antike Schlachtfelder. Bausteine zu einer antiken Kriegsgeschichte*. Leipzig: Wagner and Debes.

Labate, D., Malnati, L. and Pellegrini, S. 2012. Le mura repubblicane di Mutina. Scavi di Piazza Roma (2006-2007). *Atlante tematico di topografia antica* 22: 7-20.

Laffi, U. 1981. *Asculum II. Ricerche antiquarie e falsificazioni ad Ascoli Piceno nel secondo ottocento*. Pisa: Giardini.

Laffi, U. and Pasquinucci, M. 1975. *Asculum I*. Pisa: Giardini.

Laharnar, B. 2011. Roman lead slingshots (*glandes plumbeae*) in Slovenia. *Arheološki Vestnik* 62: 339-74.

Le Bohec, Y. 2021. *César et la guerre. Études d'histoire militaires*. Paris: Editions CNRS.

Lefebvre, B. 2018. Faire la guerre avec des mots. L'example des *glandes plumbeae*, in *Place aux Objets. Présentification et vie des artefacts en Grèce ancienne*: 215-35. Paris: L'École des Hautes Études en sciences sociales (Métis n.s.16).

Liebenam, W. 1910a. Glans, in *Realencyclopädie der classischen Altertumswissenschaft* 7: 294-296.

Liebenam, W. 1910b. Funditores, in *Realencyclopädie der classischen Altertumswissenschaft* 7: 1377-80.

Linderski. J. 1998. Updating the *CIL* for Italy: part 2. *Journal of Roman Archaeology* 11: 458-84.

Linderski, J. 2002. Romans in the province of Pesaro and Urbino. *Journal of Roman Archaeology* 15: 577-81.

López Vilar, J. 2013a. *Glandes inscriptae* a l'*ager Tarraconensis*, in J. López Vilar (ed.) *Govern i Societat a la Hispània romana. Novetats epigràfiques. Homenatge a Géza Alföldy*: 175-84. Tarragona: Fundación Privada Mútua Catalana.

López Vilar, J. 2013b. César contra Pompeyo. *Glandes inscriptae* de la batalla de Ilerda (49 aC). *Chiron* 43: 431-57.

Luik, M. 2002. *Die Funde aus den römischen Lagern um Numantia im Römisch-Germanischen Zentralmuseum.* Bonn / Mainz: Habelt.

Ma, J. 2010. A note on lead projectiles (*glandes, molybdines*) in support of sling bullets. A reply to T. Rihll. *Journal of Roman Archaeology* 23: 427-28.

Mainardis, F. 2007. Tra storia, collezionismo e falsificazione. Le ghiande missili dei Civici Musei di Trieste', in M. Mayer i Olivé, G. Baratta and A Guzmán Almagro (eds) *Acta XII congressus internationalis epigraphiae Graecae et Latinae*: 869-76. Barcelona: Institut d'Estudis Catalans.

Manfredi, V. 1975. Forum Gallorum nella topografia e nella storia. *Aevum* 49: 100-26.

Manganaro, G. 2000. Onomastica greca su anelli, pesi da telaio e glandes in Sicilia. *Zeitschrift für Papyrologie und Epigraphik* 133: 123-34.

Mangiameli, R. 2012. *Tra duces e milites. Forme di communicazione politica al tramonto della Repubblica.* Trieste: Edizioni Università di Trieste.

Marcadal, Y. Paillet, J.L, Roche-Tramier, A. and Tréziny, H. 2017. Balles de fronde anégraphiques de Petites Caisses. Annexe 7, in *Défendre un oppidum en Provence. Les Caisses de Jean-Jean à Mouriès (VIe-1er s. av. J.C.)*: 285-88. Aix-en-Provence: Editions Errance:

Marcos Carreras, E. 2017. *La Batalla de Baecula (208 Ane) Localització de la contesa i anàlisi de la participació dels foners baleàrics.* Unpublished BA dissertation, Universidad de Barcelona.

Marengo, S. M. 2015. Gaetano De Minicis, antiquario collezionista e le ghiande missili, in G. Paci (ed.) *I fratelli de Minicis, storici, archeologi e collezionisti del Fermano*: Ancona / Fermo: Deputazione di storia patria per le Marche.

Marion, J. 1960. Volubilis. Balles de fronde estampillées du Ier siècle av. J.-C., *Bulletin d'archéologie marocaine* 4: 488-90.

Martin-Kilcher, S. 2011. Römer und *gentes Alpinae* in Konflikt. Archäologische und historische Zeugnisse des 1. Jahrhundert v. Chr., in G. Moosbauer and R. Wiegels (eds) *Fines Imperii - Imperium Sine Fine?*: 27-62. Rahden, Westfalen: Marie Leidorf.

Mauné, S.C. 2012. Aux frontières des cités de Béziers, Lodève et Nîmes. La moyenne vallée de l'Hérault dans l'Antiquité. Développement économique et exploitation des territoires, in C. Besson, O. Blin and B. Triboulot (eds) *Franges urbaines, confins territoriaux: la Gaule dans l'Empire*: 507-26. Pessac: Ausonius.

Moog, F.P. 2002. Zur Traumatologie der antiken Schleuderblei. *Medizinhistorisches Journal* 37: 123-37.

Moralejo Ordax, J. and Saavedra, J.M. 2016. ¿César contra Pompeyo? Nuevos hallasgos para el estudio de la inscripción *SCAE* en las glandes de honda de *Hispania. Onoba* 4: 41-48.

Morillo, Á. and Aurrecoechea, J. (eds) 2006. *The Roman Army in Hispania. An archaeological Guide.* León: University of León.

Morillo, Á. and Sala-Sellés, F. 2019. The Sertorian Wars in the conquest of Hispania. From data to archaeological assessment, in A.P. Fitzpatrick and C. Hazelgrove (eds) *Caesar's Battle for Gaul. New archaeological Perspectives*: 49-72. Oxford: Oxbow.

Morgan, J.D. 1983. Palaepharsalus. The battle and the town. *American Journal of Archaeology* 87: 23-54.

Müller, R., 2018. *Die Bleifunde der römisch-republikanischen Anlage von Sanisera, Menorca. Archäologische und archäometrische Analyse.* Oxford: Archaeopress.

Müller, R., Brey, G.P., Seitz, H.-M. and Klein, S. 2014. Lead isotope analyses on Late Republican sling bullets. *Archaeological and Anthropological Sciences* 7: 473-85.

Münzer, F. 1918. Julius (Caesar). *Realencyclopädie der classischen Altertumswissenschaft* 10: 464-78.

Münzer, F. 1920. Salvidienus 4. *Realencyclopädie der classischen Altertumswissenschaft* 1A: 2019-21.

Noguera, J., Valdés, P., Ble, E. and López Vilar, J. 2018. Tracing the Roman Republican Army. Military Archaeology in the Northeast of the Iberian peninsula, in C.S. Sommer and S. Matešić (eds) *Limes XXIII. Proceedings of the 23rd International Limes Congress, Ingolstadt, 2015*, volume 2: 277-90. Mainz: Nünnerich-Asmus.

Noguera, J., Valdés, P. and Ble, E. 2022. New perspectives on the Sertorian War in northeastern Hispania. Archaeological surveys of the Roman camps of the lower River Ebro. *Journal of Roman Archaeology* 35: 1-32.

Olson, B.R. 2008. Aerial insults. The tradition of inscribing lead sling-bullets in antiquity. *Military History* (online blog), 12 February, 2008.

Osgood, J. 2006. *Caesar's Legacy. Civil War and the Emergence of the Roman Empire.* Cambridge: Cambridge University Press.

Paridaens, N., Salesse, K., Müller, R., Klein, S., Snoek, C. and Mattielli, N. 2020. Les balles de fronde en plomb découvertes sur l'*oppidum* de Thuin. Charactérisation, origine et interprétation. *Signa* 9: 111-23.

Parsons, A.W. 1943. Klepsydra and the paved court of the Pythion. *Hesperia* 12: 191-267.

Passelac, M. 2006. D'*Elesiodunum* à *Elusio*. Nouveaux documents sur occupation préromaine de Montferrand (Aude) et le déplacement de l'agglomération. *Bulletin de la Société d'Études Scientifiques de l'Aude* 105: 21-34.

Pelling, C.B.R. 1973. Pharsalus. *Historia* 22: 249-59.

Peralta Labrador, E.J. 2006 Guerras Cántabras en la montaña palentina. El asedio de La Loma. *Revista de Arqueología* 27: 24-33.

Perea Yébenes, S. 1997 Dos nuevas *glandes inscriptae* de la provincia de Córdoba. *Arx* 2-3 (1996-1997): 167-72.

Pérez Gutiérrez, M.L. 2014. Tras las huellas de Sertorio en Hispania. Arqueología de la primera guerra civil romana (82-72 a.c.). Unpublished MA dissertation, Universidad de Cantabria.

Pernet, L., Poux, M. and Teegen, W.-R. 2008. Militaria gaulois et romaines sur l'oppidum de Bibracte, Mont-Beuvray (Nièvre), in M. Poux (ed.) *Sur les traces de César. Militaria tardo-républicains en contexte gaulois*: 103-39. Glux-en-Glenne: Bibracte, Centre Archéologique européen.

Petersen, E., von Domaszewski, A. and Calderini, G. 1896. *Die Marcus-Säule auf Piazza Colonna in Rom.* München: Bruckmann.

Pimenta, J., Henriques, E. and Mendes, H. 2012. *O Acampamento de Alto dos Cacos – Almeirim.* Almeirim: Câmara municipal.

Pina Polo, F. and Zanier, W. 2006. *Glandes inscriptae* procedentes de la Hispania Ulterior. *Archivo Español de Arqueología* 79: 29-50.

Pina Polo, F. and Zanier, W. 2009. *Glandes inscriptae* aus der Hispania Ulterior, in Á. Morillo, N. Hanel and E. Martín (eds) *Limes XX. Estudios sobre la frontera romana* (Anejos de Gladius 13): 577-84. Madrid: Ediciones Polifemo.

Planes Palau, A. and Madrid Aznar, J. 1994. *La útil honda balear nutrida de plomo*. Ibiza: "Sa Nostra" Caixa de Balears.

Polita, E. 2007. *Studio e catalogazione delle ghiande missili in piombo della Collezione Civica del Museo Archeologico Statale di Ascoli Piceno*. Unpublished dissertation, Università di Macerata.

Poux, M. 2000 Les frondeurs de César. *L'Archéologe* 48: 34-36.

Poux, M. 2008. L'empreinte du militaire tardo-républicain dans les faciès mobiliers de La Tène finale, in M. Poux (ed.) *Sur les Traces de César. Militaria césariens en contexte gaulois*: 299-432. Glux-en-Glenne: Bibracte, Centre Archéologique Européen.

Poux, M., Feugère, M. and Demierre, M. 2008. Autour de Gergovie. Les militaria, découvertes anciennes et recentes, in M. Poux (ed.) *Sur les Traces de César. Militaria césariens en contexte gaulois*: 203-24. Glux-en-Glenne: Bibracte, Centre Archéologique Européen.

Poux, M. and Guyard, L. 1999. Un moule à balles de fronde inscrit d'époque tardo-républicaine à Paris (rue Saint-Martin). *Instrumentum* 9: 29-30.

Poux, M. and Robin, S. 2000. Les origins de Lutèce. Acquis chronologiques. Nouveaux indices d'une présence militaire à Paris, rive gauche. *Gallia* 57: 181-225.

Pritchett, W.K. 1991. *The Greek State at War*, volume 5. Berkeley / Los Angeles / Oxford: University of California Press.

Pujol, Á., Fernández-Götz, M., Sala, R., Padrós, C., Ble, E., Tamba, R. and Rubio-Campillo, X. 2019. The archaeology of the Roman civil wars. The destruction of Puig Ciutat (Catalonia, Spain) and Caesar's campaign in Ilerda (49 B.C.), in A.P. Fitzpatrick and C. Hazelgrove (eds) *Caesar's Battle for Gaul. New archaeological Perspectives*: 227-50. Oxford: Oxbow.

Quesada Sanz, F. 2008. Armamento romano e ibérico en 'Urso' (Osuna). Testimonio de una época. *Cuadernos de los Amigos de los Museos de Osuna* 10: 13-19.

Quesada Sanz, F., Gómez Cabeza, F., Molinos Molinos, M. and Bellón Ruiz, J.P. 2015. El armamento hallado en el campo de batalla de Las Albahacas – Baecula, in J.P. Bellón, A. Ruiz, M. Molinos, C. Rueda and F. Gómez (eds) *La Segunda Guerra Púnica en el Península Ibérica. Baecula. Arqueología de una batalla*: 311-96. Jaén: Universidad de Jaén.

Rageth, J., Zanier, W. and Klein, S. 2010. Crap Ses und Septimer. Archäologische Zeugnisse der römischen Alpeneroberung 16/15 v. Chr. aus Graubünden. *Germania* 88: 241-83.

Raggi, A. 2014. Storia di Ascoli in età repubblicana, in G. Paci (ed.) *Storia di Ascoli dai Piceni all'epoca romana*: 85-105. Ascoli Piceno: Librati.

Reddé, M. 2019. Recent archaeological research on Roman military engineering works of the Gallic War, in A.P. Fitzpatrick and C. Hazelgrove (eds) *Caesar's Battle for Gaul. New archaeological Perspectives*: 91-112. Oxford: Oxbow.

Reid, J.H. and Nicholson, A. 2019. Burnswark Hill. The opening shot of the Antonine reconquest of Scotland? *Journal of Roman Archaeology* 32: 459-77.

Reid, J.H., Müller, R. and Klein, S. 2022. The Windridge Farm *glandes* revisited. Clues to conquest? *Britannia* 53: 323-46.

Rihll, T. 2009. Lead slingshot (*glandes*). *Journal of Roman Archaeology* 22: 146-69.

Robinson, D.M. 1942. *Excavations at Olynthus. Part 10. Metal and minor miscellaneous Finds. An original Contribution to Greek Life*. Baltimore: Johns Hopkins.

Rohr Vio, F. 1999. Autocensura e storiografia augustea: il caso di Salvidieno Rufo. *Prometheus* 23.1: 27-39.

Rolland, H. 1951. *Fouilles de Saint-Blaise (Bouches du Rhône)*. Paris: Centre national de la recherche scientifique.

Rothenhöfer, P. 2018. Ein epigraphisches Zeugnis aus den Sklavenkriegen Roms. *Hermes* 146: 290-97.

Rowan, C. 2019. *From Caesar to Augustus (c. 49 BC-AD 14). Using coins as Sources*. Cambridge: Cambridge University Press.

Roymans, N. 2019. Caesar's conquest and the archaeology of mass violence in the frontier zone, in A.P. Fitzpatrick and C. Hazelgrove (eds) *Caesar's Battle for Gaul. New archaeological Perspectives*: 113-33. Oxford: Oxbow.

Roymans, N. and Fernández-Götz, M. 2015. Caesar in Gaul. New perspectives on the archaeology of mass violence. *Theoretical Roman Archaeology Conference* 24: 70-80.

Ruiz Cecilia, J.I. 2015 *Urso (Osuna). Estudio y gestión de un yacimento archeológico*. Unpublished Ph.D. dissertation, Universidad de Sevilla.

Russo, F. and Russo, F. 2005. *89 a.C. Assedio a Pompei. La dinamica e le tecnologie belliche della conquista sillana di Pompei*. Pompei: Flavius.

Saddington, D.B. 1982 *The Development of the Roman Auxiliary Forces from Caesar to Vespasian (49 BC-AD 79)*, Harare: University of Zimbabwe.

Sampson, G. 2022 *The Battle of Dyrrhachium (48 BC). Caesar, Pompey and the early Campaigns of the Third Roman Civil War*. Barnsley: Pen and Sword.

Santangelo, F. 2018. The Social War, in G.D. Farney and G.J. Bradley (eds) *The Peoples of Ancient Italy*: 231-54. Berlin / Boston: De Gruyter.

Schinco, G. and Small, A. 2020. A previously unknown siege of Botromagno / Silvium. The evidence of slingshots from Gravina in Puglia (Provincia di Bari, Puglia). *Papers of the British School at Rome* 88: 67-118.

Schlott, C. 1999. *Zum ende des spätlatènezeitlichen Oppidum auf dem Dünsberg*. Montagnac: Éditions Monique Mergoil.

Schulten, A. 1927. *Numantia III. Die Lager des Scipio*. München: Bruckmann.

Schulten, A. 1931. *Numantia II. Die Stadt Numantia*. München: Bruckmann.

Schmitthenner, W.C.G. 1958. *The Armies of the Triumviral Period. A Study of the Origins of the Roman Imperial Legions*. Unpublished DPhil. dissertation, University of Oxford.

Scullard, H.H. 1974 *The Elephant in the Greek and Roman World*. London: Thames and Hudson.

Sheppard, S. 2006. *Pharsalus 48 B.C. Caesar and Pompey, Clash of the Titans*. Oxford: Osprey.

Sheppard, S. 2008. *Philippi 42 BC*. Oxford: Osprey.

Sievers, S. 1996. Armes Celtiques, Germaniques et Romaines. Ce que nous apprennent les fouilles d'Alésia, in M. Reddé (ed.) *L'Armée romaine en Gaule*: 67-81. Paris: Errance.

Sievers, S. 2001. Les armes d'Alésia, in M. Reddé and S. von Schnurbein (eds) *Alésia. Fouilles et recherches franco-allemandes sur les travaux militaires romains autour du Mont-Auxois, 1991-1997. Tome 2, Le matériel*: 121-291. Paris: Académie des inscriptions et belles-lettres.

Sievers, S. 2007. Waffen und Kleinfunde aus Alésia. Möglichkeiten der Interpretation, in S. von Schnurbein and M. Reddé (eds) *Alésia et la bataille du Teutoburg*: 245-59. Ostfildern: Thorbecke.

Simonett, C. 1947. *Führer durch das Vindonissa-Museum in Brugg*. Brugg: Effingerhof.

Small, A. and Small, C. 2022. *Archaeology on the Apulian-Lucanian Border*. Oxford: Archaeopress.

Smallwood, E.M. 1966. *Documents illustrating the Principates of Nerva, Trajan and Hadrian*. Cambridge: Cambridge University Press.

Smith, C. 1998. Onasander on how to be a general, in M. Austin, J. Harries and C. Smith (eds) *Modus Operandi. Essays in Honour of Geoffrey Rickman*: 151-66. London: Institute of Classical Studies.

Solari, A. 1939. Forum Gallorum. *Athenaeum* 17: 386-90.

Sovernigo, P.G. 2018. Le ghiande missili di Adria. *Quaderni Friulani di Archeologia* 28: 97-106.

Speidel, M.P. 1989. The soldiers' servants. *Ancient Society* 20: 239-48 = M.P. Speidel, *Roman Army Studies* 2, 1992: 342-352. Stuttgart: Steiner.

Starr, C.G. 1941. *The Roman Imperial Navy*. Ithaca: Cornell University Press.

Stenhouse, W. 2002. *The Paper Museum of Cassiano dal Pozzo. Ancient Inscriptions*. London: Harvey Miller.

Stiebel, G. 1997. 'You were the word of war.' A sling shot testimony from Israel. *Journal of Roman Military Equipment Studies* 8: 301-07.

Thorburn, J.E. 2003. Lixae and calones. Following the Roman army. *Classical Bulletin* 79: 47-61.

Ulbert, G. 1984. *Cáceres el Viejo. Ein spätrepublikanisches Legionslager in Spanisch-Extremadura*. Mainz: von Zabern.

Unzueta Portilla, M. 2006. Andagoste battlefield, in Á. Morillo and J. Aurrecoechea (eds) *The Roman Army in Hispania. An Archaeological Guide*: 218-21. León: University of León.

Veith, G. 1920. *Die Feldzug von Dyrrhachium zwischen Caesar und Pompejus*. Wien: Seidel.

Velaza Frías, J., Cinca Martínez, J.L., Ramírez Sábada, J.L. 2003. Nuevo testimonio de las guerras sertorianas en Calahorra. Un depósito de projectiles de catapulta. *Kalakoricos* 8: 9-30.

Verdin, F. 2013. Marcus Agrippa et l'Aquitaine. *Aquitania* 29: 69-104.

Vicente, J.P., Punter, M.P. and Ezquerra, B. 1997. La catapulta tardo-republicana y otro equipamiento militar de La Caridad (Caminreal, Teruel). *Journal of Roman military Equipment Studies* 8: 167-99.

Vitelli Casella, M. 2019. Qualche considerazione storica sulle ghiande missili di Ossero / Osor. In margine a CIL I^2 887, 888. *Epigraphica* 81: 697-708.

Völling, T. 1990. Funditores im römischen Heer. *Saalburg Jahrbuch* 45: 24-58.

Von Bothmer, D. 1957. *Amazons in Greek Art*. Oxford: Clarendon Press.

Walker, S. and Higgs, P. (eds) 2001. *Cleopatra of Egypt, from History to Myth*. London: British Museum Press.

Wallmann, P. 1975. Untersuchungen zu militärischen Problemen des Perusinischer Krieges. *Talanta* 6: 58-91.

Wild, J.P. 1998. A sling from Melandra?, in J. Bird (ed.) *Form and Fabric. Studies in Rome's material Past in Honour of B.R. Hartley*: 297-300. Oxford: Oxbow.

Wilkins, A. 2017. *Roman Imperial Artillery*. Dumfries: Solway Print.

Zandstra, M.J.M. 2019. *Miles away from Home. Material Culture as a Guide to the Composition and Deployment of the Roman Army in the Lower Rhine Area during the First Century A.D.* Unpublished PhD dissertation, University of Nijmegen.

Zangemeister, K.F. 1885. *Glandes plumbeae Latine inscriptae* (Ephemeris Epigraphica 6). Berlin: Reimer.

Zucca, R. 1998. *Insulae Baliares. Le isole Baleari sotto il dominio romano.* Roma: Carocci.

Index

A
Actium, battle of, 65
Aemilius Lepidus, M. (Triumvir), 50
Aemilius Lepidus, M. (supporter of Q. Sertorius), 26
Aemilius Paullus, L., 76
Aetolians, 10, 12; Figure 13.3
Afranius, L., 35
Agedincum, 31
Agen, L'Ermitage d', 64
Agrippa, *see* Vipsanius Agrippa
Alesia, 31; Figure 15
Alexandria, 42
Alpenfeldzug, Der, 66
Altès, 31
Alto dos Cacos, 46
Amazon warrior, 4
Andagoste, 64
Antiochus III, Seleucid king, 76
Antonius, L., 47, 53-54, 56, 58, 60-61, 79; Figures 34-35
Antonius, M. (Mark Antony), 33, 47-50, 53-54, 57-58, 64-65, 80; Figures 18.5, 32.4, 37
Antonius Hermeros, M., 66; Figure 38
Apidius, 8, 57, 79; Figure 32.7
Apsorus, 64
Aquitania, 64
Arausio, 31 footnote 52
archers, 31, 35, 41-42, 52, 65, 71, 74-75
Asculum, 8, 15-19, 74, 77-80; Figures 8-10
Aspendus, 4; front cover
Asso, 46
Astigi, 44, 47
Ategua, 42, 44
Athens, 23
Atuatuci, 30
Augustus (Roman emperor), 3, 47, 66, 80; *see also* Octavian
Azuaga, 27

B
Baecula, 78
Baeterrae, 52
Balearic Islands, 3, 8, 10, 30
Balearic slingers, 3-4, 10, 24, 30, 35, 71, 79
ballista balls, 12, 23, 26, 31, 44, 65, 73; Figure 6
Beius, T., 46
Benedetti, L., 16, 53
Bibracte, 30
Bocchus, king of Mauretania, 33
Bononia, 47
Bordeaux, 64
Botromagno, 30
Britain, Caesar's invasion of, 31
Brundisium, 35, 77
Burnswark, 4, 8, 75
Byzantium, 40

C
Cáceres el Viejo, 26
Caecilius Metellus Baliaricus, Q., 10
Caecilius Metellus Creticus, Q., 30
Caecilius Metellus Pius, Q., 24, 27, 37
Caesar, *see* Julius Caesar
Calabria, 50
Calagurris, 26
Campania, 47
Cannae, battle of, 76-77
Caridad, La, 26
Carrhae, battle of, 30, 64
Carthago Nova, 26
Cassius Longinus, C., 52
Castellano, River, 15, 19; Figure 8
Castra Martia, 26
catapult, 26, 35
Celsus, A. Cornelius, 76
centurions named on bullets, 9, 57, 78
Cephaloedium, 62
Cerro de las Balas, 8, 44-45

Cicero, Q. Tullius, 7
Claudius (emperor), 66
Claudius Quadrigarius, Q., 75
Cleopatra, 42
Cloche, La, 35
coins, Figures 11, 22, 26, 28, 29, 34, 36-37; front cover
Commagenorum, Cohors VI, 71
Corduba, 44
Cornelius Scipio Aemilianus, P., 12
Cornelius Sulla, L., 23, 80; Figure 11
Corropoli, 19
Crete, 30, 41, 78

D
Dacia, 68
David (shepherd boy), 4, 76
De Minicis, G., 2
De Munitionibus Castrorum, 71
Dertosa, 37
Domitius Ahenobarbus, Altar of, Figure 2
Drusus (brother of Tiberius), 66
Dyrrhachium, 37, 39-41, 77; Figure 24

E
elephants, 12, 31, 42; Figure 22
Epitynchanus, 66; Figure 38
Etrius, T., 57

F
Fabricius, T., 57
Falconer, Rev. W., 52
Feridius, M., 57; Figure 33.3
Firmum, 15, 18, 80; Figure 9.6
Fortnum, C.D.E., 52, 57
Forum Gallorum, 48
Fretum Siculum, 51
Fulvia, 54, 58-60; Figure 32.1
funditores, 2

G
Gabrielli, G., 15, 19
Galatians, 76
Garonne, River, 64

Gaul, Cisalpine, 35, 47
Gaul, Transalpine, 31
Gergovia, 30
Glons, 53
graffiti, 80

H
Hannibal, 3, 10, 77
Hatria (Adria), 2 footnote 6
Hatria (Atri), 31
Herculaneum, 80
Herod Agrippa II, king, 76
hillforts, Iron Age, 4, 64, 66, 75
Hirtius, A., 47, 49

I
Ibiza, 10, 30, 79
Ilerda, battle of, 35, 37-39

J
Jerusalem, 76
Jewish War, 66, 76
Josephus, 76
Jugurtha, 10, 12
Julius Caesar, C. (dictator), 7, 10, 30-31, 33, 35, 38-45, 47, 56, 64; Figures 22, 26
Julius Caesar, C. (Julius Caesar's adopted son); *see* Octavian
Julius Caesar, Sex., 38
Junius Brutus, Dec., 47
Junius Brutus, M., 52

L
Labienus, T., 31, 42; Figure 18.2
Lafrenius, T., 19; Figure 9.2
Lambaesis, 7, 71
Lantejuela, 44, 46
Larissa, 41
Lautagne, 30 footnote 32
lead
    bullets, *passim*
    ingots, 7
    isotope analysis, 8, 79
legions
    II, 48

II *Pansiana*, 47
IIII (IV), 47, 57
V, 57; Figure 37
V *Alaudae*, 47
VI, 37, 54, 57, 79; Figure 32.7
VII, 47, 54
VIII, 47
VIII *Mutinensis*, 47
VIIII (IX), 18
X, 51-52
X *Equestris*, 57
X *Fretensis*, 51-52
XI, 54, 57; Figures 33.3, 5
XII, 37, 54; Figure 32.8
XII *Victrix*, 54; Figure 32.6
XII *Gallica*, 56 footnote 21
XIII, 43, 45, 66
XV, 18, 43, 57; Figures 9.4-5
XXXV, 47
XLI, 9
Legio Firma, 43
Leosthenes, 76
Liberators, The, 47, 52
Licinius Crassus, M., 64
Licinius Lucullus, L., 30
lightning-bolt, 7, 9, 23, 31, 33, 51, 58; Figures 13.2, 29, 32.1, 3
Lilybaeum, 62
Lippe, River, 66
Lomba do Canho, 4, 26
lufinasia, 8, 57; Figure 33.4
Lygdamus, 35

M
Macedonia, 40, 47, 76
Mago, 3
Mallorca, 10, 75
Manlius, L., 31, 33
Marcus Column, Rome, 71; Figure 42
Mark Antony, *see* Antonius, M.
Massilia, 31, 35-36
Mauretania, 33
Menorca, 8, 10, 32, 79
Mommsen, T., 15
Montagne Sainte-Geneviève, 31
Monte Bernorio, 78
Monteluce, 53
Montferrand, 53, 61
moulds for making sling bullets 7, 9; Figure 4
Munda, battle of, 42, 44-45, 78-79
Museums
    Arqueológico de Osuna, Figure 1
    Arqueológico de Sevilla, 35, 37
    Archeologico Nazionale dell'Umbria, Perugia, 53
    Archeologico Statale, Ascoli, 16, 20; Figure 10
    Ashmolean, University of Oxford, 52-53, 57
    della Civiltà Romana, Rome, Figure 10
    Hunterian, University of Glasgow, Figures 11, 22, 26, 28-29, 36-37
    Nazionale Romano, Rome, 16, 53
Mutina, 47-49; Figure 27
Mylae, 64

N
Narbo Martius, 52
Naulochus, 64
Nemausus, 52
Nervii, 7
Nile, River, 42
Numantia, 7, 10-13, 78, 80; Figures 3, 5-6

O
Octavian (later Augustus), 47, 50, 53-54, 58-59, 61, 64-65, 79-80; Figures 28, 32.5, 33.1, 35
Olynthus, 46 fn. 69
Onasander, 74-76
Opitergium, 18, 77; Figure 9.3

P
Paestum, 7, 23, 77
Paris, 7, 31
Parma, 47
Parthians, 65, 75

Perperna, M., 30
Perusia, 8, 19, 51, 53-61; Figures 31-33, 35
Petites Caisses de Mouriès, 31
Petreius, M., 35, 42
phallus, 58-59; Figure 33.6
Pharsalus, battle of, 39, 41, 74
Philippi, battle of, 50, 52, 57, 64
Picamoixons, 35
Pisaurum, 31
Polita, E., 16
Pompeii, 23, 77-78, 80; Figure 12
Pompeius Magnus, Cn. (The Great), 42
Pompeius Magnus, Cn. (The Younger), 7, 43; Figures 1, 20.3
Pompeius Magnus, Sex., 43-45, 50, 62; Figure 36
Pompeius Strabo, Cn., 18-19; Figure 9.1
Prades, 37
Praeneste, 60
primus pilus, 37, 41, 57, 82
Ptolemy XIII, king of Egypt, 42
Puebla de Cazalla, La, 46
Puig Ciutat, 35

R
Rhine, River, 66
Rhithymna, 30
Rubicon, River, 35
Ruf... , M., 18; Figure 9.4
Ruspina, 42

S
Saint-Affrique, 31
Saint-Blaise, 31
Saint-Pargoire, 52
Salvidienus Rufus, Q., 8, 50-52, 54, 58, 78; Figures 18.7, 29, 32.3
San Pietro, Abbey of, 58; Figure 31
Sanisera, 10
Scaeva, 31, 41, 57, 78; Figure 32.8
Scaevola, P. Mucius, 38
Schulten, A., 12-13
Sertorius, Q., 23-26, 30, 42, 80; Figure 13.1

Seville, 44
Sicily, 42, 50-52, 62; Figure 30
sieges, 12-13, 15-20, 23, 26, 31, 35-36, 44, 47, 49, 53-61, 64, 75-79
slaves, 19, 23
sling bullets
   clay, 7; Figure 3
   lead, 7-9
   stone, 4
   and *passim*
slings, 4
Slovenia, 64
Social War, 1, 10, 15, 23, 77
Sosus, king of Mauretania, 33; Figure 13.2
Spartacus, 30
Syria, 39, 64

T
Tarraco, 36-38
Tauromenium, 50
Teanum, 47
Thamusida, 33
Thermopylae, 76
Thessalonica, 40
Thrace, 41, 78
throwing of stones, 5, 7, 71, 73; Figures 39-40
Thuin, 30
Tiberius (emperor), 66
Tigranocerta, 30
Tortoreto, 19
Trajan's Column, Rome, 68, 73; Figures 39-41
Tres Cales, Les, 26
tribunus militum, 38, 57, 62, 80
Triumvirate, Second, 50
Tronto, River, 15
Tyrrhenus, 35

U
Ufinius Asia..., L., 58
Ulia, 43
Urso, 44, 46 footnote 69

V
Valentia (Valence, France), 30
Valentia (Valencia, Spain), 26
Varius, C., 52; Figure 18.6
Varro, C., 52
Velsen, 8
Vergina, 76
Via Egnatia, 40
Vipsanius Agrippa, M., 54, 64, 80; Figure 18.8
Vibius Pansa, C., 47-49
Vibo Valentia, 50
Völling, T., 2, 7, 15, 79
Völling's Types, 2

Z
Zangemeister, K., 15, 19, 53, 58